Presented To:

From:

Date:

Healing in the Hurting Places

KAREN F. RILEY

© Copyright 2011–Karen F. Riley

All rights reserved. This book is protected by the copyright laws of the United States of America. This book may not be copied or reprinted for commercial gain or profit. The use of short quotations or occasional page copying for personal or group study is permitted and encouraged. Permission will be granted upon request. Unless otherwise identified, Scripture quotations are taken from the New King James Version. Copyright © 1982 by Thomas Nelson, Inc. Used by permission. All rights reserved. Scripture quotations marked NIV are taken from the HOLY BIBLE, NEW INTERNATIONAL VERSION®, Copyright © 1973, 1978, 1984 International Bible Society. Used by permission of Zondervan. All rights reserved. Scripture quotations marked NASB are taken from the NEW AMERICAN STANDARD BIBLE®, Copyright © 1960, 1962, 1963, 1968, 1971, 1972, 1973, 1975, 1977, 1995 by The Lockman Foundation. Used by permission. Scripture quotations marked NLT are taken from the Holy Bible, New Living Translation, copyright 1996, 2004. Used by permission of Tyndale House Publishers, Wheaton, Illinois 60189. All rights reserved. Scripture quotations marked HCSB are taken from the Holman Christian Standard Bible Copyright © 1999, 2000, 2002, 2003 by Holman Bible Publishers, Nashville, Tennessee. Used by permission. All rights reserved. Please note that Destiny Image's publishing style capitalizes certain pronouns in Scripture that refer to the Father, Son, and Holy Spirit, and may differ from some publishers' styles. Take note that the name satan and related names are not capitalized. We choose not to acknowledge him, even to the point of violating grammatical rules.

DESTINY IMAGE® PUBLISHERS, INC.

P.O. Box 310, Shippensburg, PA 17257-0310

"Promoting Inspired Lives"

This book and all other Destiny Image, Revival Press, MercyPlace, Fresh Bread, Destiny Image Fiction, and Treasure House books are available at Christian bookstores and distributors worldwide.

For a U.S. bookstore nearest you, call 1-800-722-6774.

For more information on foreign distributors, call 717-532-3040.

Reach us on the Internet: www.destinyimage.com.

ISBN 13 TP: 978-0-7684-3888-8

ISBN 13 Ebook: 978-0-7684-8961-3

For Worldwide Distribution, Printed in the U.S.A.

1 2 3 4 5 6 7 8 9 10 11 / 13 12 11

Dedicated to all who have suffered from the pain of childhood sexual abuse…

To those who love them and want to be part of their healing journey…

And to my Lord and Savior, who has set this captive free.

Acknowledgments

I love to travel. I enjoy hopping into my car and heading out toward places unknown, places waiting to be discovered. I've always enjoyed opening up a road map and surveying the area—the curving streets, the roads that dead-end next to a lake, those interesting sites with brief notations begging to be explored.

And it's a cool thing for me to stumble across a road I have been on before or learn how a highway in an unknown part of the state connects to another I'm familiar with. But the best part is to open a map and recognize all of the spots that I have already visited and recall the memories. What were the feelings as I journeyed there for the first time? Was I excited about what I might find there? Tired from the day's journey and not really caring about anything other than finding some rest for the night? Was I disappointed that my discovery did not match my expectations?

I often look back on my life in the same fashion. Only now, I can see how God intersected all of those points for His purposes. The times I thought I was lost, actually served to draw me closer to Him.

My greatest disappointments may have led to my greatest lessons. And too often, the stops along the way that I enjoyed so much were only seasons in His timing—and all too quickly, I had to move on to the next stop on the journey.

I've met so many people along the way. Isn't it funny how sometimes the people who have such an impact may be in our lives for only a brief time? Too often, we don't even realize until much later the effect they had on us. I feel blessed to have been able to go back and track down some of those folks and let them know how they have changed my life for the better. Sadly, some of them passed on before I could acknowledge the role they had played.

But just like that curving road that we cross again further along in our travels, I am grateful that God has brought my life full circle in so many ways. I've had opportunities to relive certain moments, connect with old friends, or do things I thought had passed me by for good. God has been so gracious to me and in so many ways. He has provided me with more than I could have ever wished for.

The beginning of my journey may have had a few bumps in the road and even a pothole or two, but at least I know where the road will end and how joyous that time will be! I look forward to being reunited with all of the people I've encountered on my journey and having all of eternity to spend with them. I can't wait to open that road map again with the understanding of why God had put me in that particular spot with certain people during a time He appointed. Even now, with the wisdom of hindsight, some of those detours make perfect sense, and I appreciate the danger zones He kept me out of many times.

I have so much to be thankful for and so many people I am indebted to. There are many people who stood by me when they could have walked away…spoke the truth in love when keeping silent would have been easier…or gave me a second, third, or fourth chance. There are people I've hurt—sometimes too many times to count—who continued to love me and forgive me. There are those who were hurting also, who came alongside and journeyed with me, and together we bore each other's burdens.

There were times when I drove too fast and missed out on some wonderful things—many of which I can't revisit. There are times when I drove with blinders on, seeing only what I wanted to see on my travels. And there are mercifully times when I could return again and do things differently on the subsequent visit.

Too many times, I didn't like the place I was in and couldn't wait to get to where I wanted to go. I had to learn the hard way that God had His reasons for the delay, and many times it was my stubbornness to not see why I was in that place that kept me from moving ahead as quickly as I would have liked.

Quite honestly, some of those places brought me pain, and I wished I had never been there. But those places also enabled me to become the person God had for me all along. They have enriched and brought me relationships that I would not have had were it not for those dark places.

There are places on the map that I still hope to see some day. I may get there and I may not. I am learning to be content in where I am for this moment and to look forward with excitement, knowing that what God has planned for me will be far better than anything I could have envisioned.

Still, there is sadness for those who are no longer part of my journey, for those who have passed on, left or never understood. Like the heavy snorer or the person who over-packs, I have not been the easiest person to travel with. My vehicle has seen a lot of mileage and there are a lot of dents to show for those miles.

But I know I would not have traded this journey for anything. It has been a privilege to have traveled this path. Those who shared it with me have blessed my life in immeasurable ways.

I will always be thankful to the One who was really behind the wheel the whole time..the One who guided my journey...the One who kept me safe....

> *Trust in the LORD with all your heart,*
> *And lean not on your own understanding;*
> *In all your ways acknowledge Him,*
> *And He shall direct your paths* (Proverbs 3:5-6).

Endorsements

Your book was very moving, Karen. Some parts were easier for me to read than others, but all of them, in one way or another, rang true for me. Thanks for being brave enough to write it.

Jeffrey Russell, a sexual abuse survivor

Thank you for sharing your story and for the awesome privilege of being able to read it. I was blessed by virtually every page. I was also struck by precisely how on-target your assessments were of PTSS victims' behavior as borne out in the experience of several people I have worked with over the years. Thank you for the courage to write this book and for all the ministry that will definitely come from this labor of love. Thanks again for being such an awesome inspiration of what God can do in all things!

Pastor Scott Hoffman,
Ocean Grove Camp Meeting Association CEO

I just want to tell you how much I admire your courage and your ability to give voice to your experience. I was moved by many of the incidents you shared and I am sure other readers will be, too.

BJH

I thought it was an amazing book. I cried a few times and in a lot of weird ways, I related to a lot of your thoughts and feelings, though I know I could never understand what it is like to have gone through what you did. I've had times when I've felt some of the things you've felt, and I think a lot of people will have that and be able to relate in some way, even if they haven't experienced what you have. Having it touch me that much makes me sure that it must really hit home to those who have felt that exactly. I think those pieces of you and your feelings that I relate to will help all of those that you reached out to that have loved ones that have gone through it understand a little better. I think it is very important for people to find and read your book just to help them feel and understand what some people may be going through. You also showed how being a Christian can be so helpful in bringing you through the process and provide a way and an open door for people to accept Jesus into their lives and know that there is a way to get through it.

Jeremy Skillings

As a pastor I often struggle with how to connect on a level that touches and changes the very lives of those I am given to. To reach down deep into their soul and leave an eternal truth hoping that it will release some bondage holding them back from realizing the glory God has planned to draw from their life. But all the while knowing I lack something in terms of the length of my reach. I'm reminded of a quote from a Thorton Wilder play, *The Angel That Troubled the Waters*. The main character, a doctor, is seeking to be healed from his deep emotional wounds but instead hears:

'Doctor, without your wounds, where would your power be? It is your melancholy that makes your low voice tremble into the hearts of men and women. The very angels themselves cannot persuade the wretched and laundering children of this earth as can one human being broken on the wheels of living. In love's service only wounded soldiers can serve ...'

Karen's healing process has arrived at a point where telling her story and all she has learned from it can effectively bring others with similar experiences forward and closer to the wholeness she continues to grow in.

As for me, I agree with Karen that having never experienced these things I am incapable when it comes to understanding what she and others are going through. However, now that I've read her story, I am much better equipped to listen, guide, and love those searching for dawn after a life of darkness.

Pastor John Durante
Jersey Shore Calvary Chapel

Intriguingly enough, this is a personal account of hope and even gratefulness. Karen shares her intimate experience of childhood trauma whose hidden hurts act out through her teen and adult years. She gives us a peek into the reflections of her soul and the God of her universe, as well as the hurt's painful effects on relationships with peers and family. I found many "Wow" moments as Karen reveals the emotional, mental, and spiritual layers necessary to navigate the long road of her healing process. The reader will not only find compassion for the abused but will become better equipped to understand just how many aspects of a person's life this type of trauma truly can affect. And for the abused, it offers a lovingly practical and spiritual guide to recovery.

D.C., Ocean Grove

Healing in the Hurting Places guides you through Karen Riley's journey from the mental and destructive anguish of an incestuous rape, to the rebirth of her Christian values. With almost 40 years of torment, Karen is compelled to overcome the self-destruction and loss of relationships as her support from God enlightens and heals her pain. Karen's courage to share her experience demonstrates her growth as a Christian woman. I feel honored to have read it.

Maryann Kley, Farmington, NM

As a registered nurse, I know the ongoing pain of the victims of sexual abuse. Karen F. Riley reaches out to those victims with healing power. Her personal sharing and honest words make her journey to recovery a spellbinding tale. The strength of her faith and the truth of her message make *Healing in the Hurting Places* a must read for all who have suffered the tragedy of childhood abuse.

K.B., registered nurse

God continues to show Himself sovereign through this journey to redemption! Thank you, Karen, for being brave enough to share your story with the world. May this book give those who are hurting the strength to someday share their own. Through your pain, others will be pointed to the Truth in Jesus.

A. Gioulis, Neptune, NJ

I was immediately drawn into your journey of life; my heart pierced by the unraveling of pain suffered and lived out through your years. From the beginning, I found myself taking a deep breath, sighing with unbelief and yet thankful for all the Lord has done in and through your life. We have no idea and can't imagine what others have suffered even when it is humbly, courageously shared. It does, however, give a glimpse that deepens the opening of our eyes and hearts and allows us to see just a little of what others have experienced. I want to let you know how much I appreciate your willingness to share. The Lord has given you a gift in writing that will touch hearts, strengthen the downcast, and point them to Christ. I will continue to pray for you and am excited to see what and how the Lord will work through your testimony.

Sandie Merrit, Howell, NJ

Healing in the Hurting Places is an honest rendering of Karen's most painful memories and her vulnerability to those who exploited her. In her new book, Karen reveals the complex roller-coaster of emotions she struggled with, like so many other victims of childhood sexual abuse. Journey with Karen as she gives a candid account of the change she felt and shame she endured as she suffered through years of confusion hiding from demons trying to steal her light. Experience her triumph when she finally surrenders herself to the Great Healer, Jesus Christ, and finds true peace of mind and heart. Karen simply and explicitly reveals herself to the reader and shows how she was truly saved by Grace through faith. Amen!

Janet Fair, friend, Jackson, NJ

I was so moved by your work. It was heart-wrenching to read of your struggle with self-image. I can only tell you that I cried and felt the abuse done to your self-image though I was not a sexually abused child. As a childhood victim of intense verbal and emotional trauma, I could relate to the poor self-image that flavored my life decisions and all the relationships I have had. As such, parts of your book – especially the chapter on food struggles – touched me deeply. I know that this book will be a commercial success, but more importantly, it will help others work through the pain of abuse. I know that Jesus inspired this work. It will continue to reach others with His healing Spirit. It is your experience and heart that I found between the covers. I am glad that you chose not to include the details. Not only was it unnecessary, but it allowed the reader to apply the words to their own situation without comparison which would only dilute the message. It allowed me to see myself in the words that paint your life's story. You have found your ministry. Go forward with courage and faith. Reach the people who need you and Jesus in their lives. Help them *Heal in the Hurting Places*. I am very proud of you and your book.

Karen Kelly Boyce, Author

	Foreword	19
	Introduction	21
CHAPTER 1	*Why It Matters*	23
CHAPTER 2	*An Impenetrable Fortress*	29
CHAPTER 3	*The Façade Crumbles*	37
CHAPTER 4	*Isolation*	47
CHAPTER 5	*Victim Mentality*	55
CHAPTER 6	*The Cycle Continues*	65
CHAPTER 7	*Floodwaters*	73
CHAPTER 8	*Streams in the Desert*	79
CHAPTER 9	*The Potter's Wheel*	87
CHAPTER 10	*Bathed in Son Light*	99

Chapter 11	Out of the Comfort Zone 107
Chapter 12	Wrath and Forgiveness 115
Chapter 13	Transparency 123
Chapter 14	Walking in Truth. 129
Chapter 15	Eating Disorders. 137
Chapter 16	Yours in Healing. 147
Chapter 17	Fear of Success 173
Chapter 18	In Need of a Savior. 183
Appendix A	What (and What Not) to Say to a Sexual-Abuse Victim 199
Appendix B	Resources 207

Foreword

Who shall separate us from the love of Christ? Shall trouble or hardship or persecution or famine or nakedness or danger or sword?...For I am convinced that neither death nor life, neither angels nor demons, neither the present nor the future, nor any powers, neither height nor depth, nor anything else in all creation, will be able to separate us from the love of God that is in Christ Jesus our Lord (Romans 8:35,38-39 NIV).

While *Healing in the Hurting Places* is clearly a book that describes one of the most painful experiences a little girl can go through and live with into adulthood, it is also a book that chronicles God's plan for a woman He already loved, even before creation. The pain and suffering that Karen endured, and is still healing from, is only transformed into peace and joy by the One who had already suffered for her on the cross.

While her story of abuse brought tears of sadness to my eyes, it pales in comparison to the tears of joy that followed after reading that her life was turned around on a night when she was about to end it. The Lord used the simple sound of a guitar and a small but powerful

 in the Hurting Places

prayer from a stranger leading a worship service to spark a fire in her that perhaps she had never felt before. God's grace is available to all, at any moment, and He will not leave you where He found you, but will transform your mind, heart, and soul. Karen has not remained in a state of fear, depression, pain, or even anger as she has been renewed. She is encouraging many women and men to also find the healing that only God can impart.

Healing in the Hurting Places is a book that aids in the restoration of those who can relate all too well to Karen's past and present pain. Through her ministry she has already prompted many to come forward and begin their healing process by disclosing that they were also abused. This book also serves to educate those, who like me, have not faced this kind of pain, but can only sympathize with such a tragic past. In addition, I dare say that it may even transform the lives of those who have been the abusers if this book finds them.

Sonia Aufiero,
Certified Holistic Health Practitioner
and owner of Holistic Crossroads

Introduction

I quietly pulled my chair into the dinner table, taking care not to make eye contact with anyone. I ate in silence, the food tasteless. I ate just enough to avoid arousing suspicion and left the table as soon as I was done.

No one noticed. I was not surprised. But years later, I wondered how it could be that no one questioned the change in me. Would I have sensed that something was wrong if it were my daughter? I prayed to God that I would.

Actually, I'm sure that it would not have escaped me because I have developed an ability to tell when someone is in pain; I usually sense when they have been hurt. It is a scar that I will carry for the rest of my life. It is a scar that I've watched God use by placing people in my path to whom I can minister. I know and trust that He has a plan for my life. After all, some good must eventually come from being raped as a child.

This book is the story of my journey; it is one of hope and healing through the grace of God. Throughout my journey, I have tapped into scores of resources that address the different aspects of abuse. And

 in the Hurting Places

even with all of the resources available, I still meet people every day who do not understand the devastating effects of abuse. They want to understand, but they can't. This book is for them, to give them a peek into what it is like to come to terms with what happened to us as children and what the healing process looks like.

But more than that, it is for the victims, to let you know that you are not alone. I know what it was like to be alone.

From the minute I came upstairs to join the others at the dinner table, I would walk a different path. I would never be the same person I was the day before. The violation that had just taken place downstairs changed all of that. *How could the others eat as if nothing had happened?* Of course, they didn't see; they only saw what they wanted to.

I had to come to terms with accepting the deaths that occurred that day. Not only did I lose my innocence, but my childhood also died that day. The dreams I had were forever changed. I would never look at the world quite the same way again.

For a long time, I lived with the wounds. All I could see was the negative that came out of them—my distrust of others, my cynicism, my lack of hope. A new person sprung out of the old shell—one who was determined to rise above it all by pushing the pain and the wounds down deep inside that old, empty shell.

The new me would become driven, driven to succeed. I thought that if I could become someone, then I wouldn't be that dirty, unloved, abused child. I wanted to get as far away from her as I could. If I could be successful—a career woman with a husband and kids and property, then people would have to respect me. They would never consider who I might have been, where it all started. They would not question my past, look beyond the surface, or wonder who I was. They would only see the mask that I would wear for the next 30 years.

Chapter 1

Why It Matters

Close your eyes and think of the women you know—mother, sisters, aunts, cousins, girlfriends, co-workers, neighbors, acquaintances. The clerk who you always see at the grocery store. The woman at the Post Office you buy stamps from. Picture their faces; see their features clearly in your mind. Say their names as you envision each one. Now consider that one out of every four women is sexually assaulted before the age of 18.[1] Some therapists and studies put this number as high as one in three.

Now picture the men in your life—fathers, brothers, uncles, neighbors, co-workers, friends, distant relatives, maybe a boyfriend or spouse. Think of your little league coach, your pastors, the man at the hardware store that tells you which wrench you need for your plumbing. Now consider that one out of six males is sexually assaulted before the age of 18.[2]

Staggering, right? It is hard to pinpoint an exact number because 88 percent of child sexual abuse is never reported to the authorities. Of the cases that have been reported, one in every seven victims of

 in the Hurting Places

sexual assault is under the age of six.[3] One in three is under the age of twelve. We often think violent or traumatic crimes are committed by strangers, but in 90 percent of the rapes of children younger than twelve, the child knew the offender.[4]

"In the United States, 1.3 women are raped every minute.... The United States has the world's highest rape rate of the countries that publish such statistics. It's 4 times higher than Germany, 13 times higher than England, and 20 times higher than Japan."[5] It is important to note that rape is a crime of violence, not passion. It is motivated primarily by desire to control and dominate, rather than by sex.

I believe the way to turn the tide on this epidemic is through education. People need to know the facts about it and victims need to know where they can find resources to get help. Those who have not suffered from this crime need to know the symptoms and healing process of victims so they can help make the situation better, not worse. In addition, according to the Rape in America Study conducted in 1992, "An overwhelming majority of rape service agencies believe that public education about rape, and expanded counseling and advocacy services for rape victims, would be effective in increasing the willingness of victims to report rapes to the police."[6]

Chances are high that you know someone, probably several people, who have been sexually abused. They may never have told you, and you can't identify who the victims are, but you know them just the same—they are your relatives, friends, neighbors, and co-workers. An estimated 39 million survivors of childhood sexual abuse exist in America today.[7]

I attended a meeting once during which I felt prompted to share a story I had written about my abuse. Although the forum did not relate to abuse, I felt it was important to share part of my journey with these folks, even though I didn't realize *why* at the time. It seemed that God had a plan for that evening.

This was the first time I had written and read my story aloud. God gave me the courage to get through the difficult passages because the wounds had not yet begun to heal. There were five women and two men in the room the night I shared my story. When I finished reading, there was silence.

It was unnerving. I had no idea what these people were thinking and that unhinged me a bit. But I drew confidence from the strength that God had given me to share and now that I had spoken the truth aloud, there was nothing more I could do. I couldn't take back what I said.

Strangely enough, I didn't want to. Releasing that story was very freeing—and empowering in a way. And then, one of the women sitting at the table said in a halting voice, "Thank you for sharing that. I was raped by my half-brother when I was 12, and you just gave me the courage to speak out."

Thank You, God, I whispered. *So this is why You wanted me to share my story with these folks. Now this woman knows she is not alone and can begin to heal.*

I barely had time to think these thoughts when another woman at the table said, "My grandfather started abusing me when I was three. I barely remember that part because I was so young, but I was afraid to go to his house. And the abuse continued for years."

I told those gathered there that my therapist had told me that one out of every three women is sexually abused. I added, "And you can see, right in this room, there are three of us out of five."

 in the Hurting Places

From the other side of the table, another woman, looking down to avoid our eyes, said, "Make that four." And she didn't utter another word.

The more I speak out, the more I see God empowering others who may have also suffered to give voice to their past pain. Of course, I encounter many people who did not go through this trauma. They don't get it, because they have not been through it and don't understand it.

Most of the time, they react with anger, not at the victim, but at the perpetrator. The problem is that they are usually with the victim who has just shared their painful story. In return, the victim experiences the listener's anger. Depending on where the victim is in the healing process, anger could be the last emotion they are equipped to handle.

Personally, I had a lot of anger issues to deal with. Initially, I didn't even see myself as being angry over what happened, although I eventually learned that I just hadn't identified as anger that which I was feeling deep down. There are just so many emotions that need to be cycled through. This is true whether you are dealing with the trauma of sexual abuse, mourning the loss of a loved one, dealing with cancer, or contending with something else that shakes you to the core.

And those who have not suffered through abuse or tragic loss, although well-meaning, don't always know the right thing to say. They don't always understand the cycle of emotions. It can be an upsetting experience for them, as well, if they are close to someone who is coming to terms with this issue.

So I hope this book will encourage both parties—the victims and those who want to help the people in their lives who have been victimized—to understand the process better. There are many books, groups, therapists, and healed victims out there. All are resources. But

Why It Matters

in the end, they are all empowered by the only One who can heal you in the hurting places.

This book is my journey. I pray that it will help you with yours, and that you will come to know the Great Physician like never before.

ENDNOTES

1. "Adverse Childhood Experiences (ACE) Study: Prevalence of Individual Adverse Childhood Experiences," *Centers for Disease Control and Prevention,* http://www.cdc.gov/nccdphp/ace/prevalence.htm, accessed August 5, 2010.

2. Ibid.

3. Howard Snyder, U.S. Department of Justice Statistics, Office of Justice Programs, U.S. Department of Justice, *Sexual Assault of Young Children as Reported to Law Enforcement: Victim, Incident, and Offender Characteristics,* (July 2000).

4. Lawrence A. Greenfeld, Bureau of Justice Statistics, Office of Justice Programs, U.S. Department of Justice, *1997 Sex Offenses and Offenders: An Analysis of Data on Rape and Sexual Assault* (Washington, D.C.).

5. Coalition Educating About Sexual Endangerment (CEASE), "Rape Statistics," http://oak.cats.ohiou.edu/~ad361896/anne/cease/rapestatisticspage.html, accessed August 5, 2010.

6. "Rape in America," National Victim Center with Crime Victims Research and Treatment Center (1992), as reported in "American Rape Statistics," Paralumun New Age Village, http://www.paralumun.com/issuesrapestats.htm, accessed August 5, 2010.

7. G. Abel, J. Becker, M. Mittelman, J. Cunningham-Rathner, J. Rouleau, and W. Murphy (1987). "Self-reported Sex Crimes on Non-incarcerated Paraphiliacs" *Journal of Interpersonal Violence,* 2(1) (1987) 3-25.

CHAPTER 2

An Impenetrable Fortress

The day I was raped was the day my life changed forever. It took me more than 30 years to really understand and embrace that fact.

Because I was only a young child at the time, my first reaction was to go into self-defense mode. I immediately became self-conscious, believing that everyone around me would know what happened just by looking at me.

Later, this would become a self-fulfilling prophecy in the sense that my vibes—my actions, attitude, and behavior—would scream loudly to those around me that there was something different about me.

But initially, in those early days, I merely withdrew. It was as if I had joined a secret club and my young peers would no longer understand me. So I began to hang out with the senior citizens on my block. It was just easier that way.

They wanted someone to talk to and I didn't, so we made a good match. I sat quietly for hours, nodding at appropriate intervals as they

Healing in the Hurting Places

talked about their failing health, grandchildren who didn't visit, and the state of the economy.

Perhaps I served as a surrogate grandchild for the grandchildren they didn't see because they seemed to enjoy my company. I was starved for attention and grateful to receive some that did not have strings attached.

The block I grew up on was lined with apartment buildings. As a predominately Irish Catholic neighborhood in the Sixties, there were large families, some with as many as a dozen children. Many of the apartments were rent-controlled, making them ideal for senior citizens on a fixed budget.

There were always plenty of people for me to hang out with, both young and old. But I isolated myself from my peers after the violation and the few friends that I had were hurting also. They did not see anything odd about my behavior, because they were victims in their own way.

But in my second grade religion class, I learned about a very different kind of Friend named *Jesus*. The teacher told us that Jesus loved us and wanted to come live inside of us. I studied the illustrations in my book and decided that He had kind, gentle eyes that seemed to be looking back at me from the pages.

When I talked to the senior citizens, they looked right past me, into some other world that I couldn't see. I tried to avoid the looks from my friends because I was afraid of what they would see in me. But I didn't feel this way when I looked into the eyes of Jesus. I could hardly wait to make my First Holy Communion so He could move in.

Finally, the big day came. My mother fussed about me the whole time, telling me to stand up straight, walk slowly down the aisle, and not scuff my shoes. The bobby pins that held my veil in place dug into my scalp; I asked her to loosen them but she ignored me. In my hand was a little white purse containing the Holy Missal. On my feet were turned-down white lace anklet socks, tucked inside a brand-new pair of white patent leather shoes. Everything about me was pure white… on the outside.

All I wanted was for Jesus to come and live inside me. All I heard was my mother telling me to smile, don't slouch, look happy. I didn't want to *look* happy; I wanted to *feel* happy.

I had looked forward to receiving Jesus in my heart. I longed for that special time, but I did not feel any different afterward. I guessed that Jesus didn't want to live in my heart.

The day after I received my First Holy Communion, my parents held a party for me. They invited all of my relatives and my best friend, Elizabeth. I was feeling withdrawn and was not looking forward to the party. The only bright spot was that Elizabeth would be there.

Early that morning, she rang my doorbell. I was surprised to see her there at that hour. She wasn't dressed up and I sensed that something was wrong.

Elizabeth told me that she couldn't come to the party, that she was sorry and she pressed a small box into my hand and left. In tears, I opened the box. In it was a small, worn pendant, with a hole in the top for a chain, but there was no chain in the box. I shoved it into my desk drawer and fell on my bed in tears. I cried and cried as if my heart would break.

I still have the pendant that Elizabeth gave me that day. I keep it among my treasured possessions. I found out years later that the reason she could not come to my party was because her parents could not afford to give her money for a gift, so she gave me what she had.

Healing in the Hurting Places

Elizabeth's father was an alcoholic who could not hold down a job. Her life was also filled with pain, albeit a different kind of pain. She was hurting, just as I was.

I couldn't see that and didn't understand it at the time. All I cared about was my own breaking heart. I cried in the solitude of my bedroom and poured out my pain. I would not let my heart be vulnerable again.

After I had been raped, I knew I needed to be strong to survive and get past it. Our instinct to survive is the strongest urge God created in us. I saw weakness as counterproductive and would no longer allow myself to cry for any reason—not when my dog was put to sleep, not even when my beloved grandfather passed away.

I became driven and saw success as my ticket to freedom. For a second grade composition on what we wanted to be when we grew up, I set my sights high. I wanted to be married with three children (two girls and a boy), own a farm, become a nurse, be a writer, and have my own business. By the grace of God, I have been blessed with all but the nursing degree. I realize that desire sprung out of my need to heal the hurting, although I did not see that at the time and wouldn't have admitted it if I did.

In high school, we were required to attempt two majors and successfully complete one for graduation. I completed four, earned twice the number of credits needed, and graduated second in my class of 505 students. It was still not enough.

Burned out, I opted to enter the workforce instead of going to college, giving up the scholarship I had earned.

My intense drive, coupled with my desire to isolate myself, kept most people at bay and that was fine by me. While my co-workers would go out to lunch together, I would sit alone in my car, stuffing candy bars down my throat as I plotted my path up the corporate ladder.

At work, I was detail-oriented, exacting, and determined. I was a workaholic who thought nothing about putting in 60- to 70-hour workweeks, despite having a family at home.

I treated my subordinates with kindness, providing them with the tools, training, and resources they needed to excel. I made a point of telling them when they did a good job. I showed my appreciation by offering flexible work schedules and time off; I treated them the way I would like to have been treated.

I, on the other hand, was my own worst enemy. I strove for nothing less than 100 percent accuracy whenever possible, beat myself up on the littlest failures or problems (regardless of whether I was responsible), and constantly pushed myself to work harder and do more.

Almost 20 years later, I enrolled in college, earning a bachelor's degree in three years with a 3.86 GPA, all the while working a full-time job and raising a family. I agonized over the grades when I failed to get an "A."

I was striving for perfection, driving myself and everyone around me crazy in an attempt to achieve—and all because deep down inside I felt dirty. The grueling schedule I kept was really a way of punishing myself because I hated who I was.

I may have been kind and generous to my subordinates, but those closer to me saw a different person. I'm ashamed to look back at the person I was. Demanding, angry, opinionated—I was not open-minded or flexible. Everything had to be my way.

Nowhere was this more evident than at home. God has blessed me with an incredible husband who withstood years of my stubborn,

Healing in the Hurting Places

childish behavior because he loved me and saw a better person inside, one who was invisible to me.

There wasn't anything I liked about myself—not my face, my figure, or my voice. I lived my life attempting to prove I was somebody because deep inside, I felt like nobody.

My children also got the short end of the stick. I will always regret that I was not the person I could or should have been for my family. I tried to be a good mother; I enrolled my kids in all kinds of activities: swimming, tennis, ice skating, gymnastics, ballet, softball, basketball, archery, soccer, bowling, Boy Scouts, Girl Scouts, even baton twirling for my daughters. I was a co-leader for both the Boy Scout and Girl Scout troops; I was also the class mother, the coach's wife, and our block association president.

We baked cookies at Christmas, went sledding in the winter, and took hikes in the spring. My husband and I instilled the love of nature into our children and exposed them to literature and civics.

Here's what I *wasn't:* emotionally available to my children. It was all window dressing, like the way I treated my subordinates. I put on this mask and did the right thing in public because that's all I could do. As much as I wanted to be a nurturing mother, it wasn't in me to give. If you hate yourself, you cannot truly love others.

I also wasn't domesticated. Cleaning was not my strength. I came from a home that was spotlessly clean, so everything looked great on the outside, but was anything but great underneath. Because this was so blatantly obvious to me, I believe I rebelled against it by maintaining a "lived-in" look. The trouble was that my actions were about appearances on the outside, while inside I was a mess. I just chose a different way to act it out.

An Impenetrable Fortress

Another barrier to my well-kept home was the fact that I was a closet pack rat, holding onto scraps of paper in the event that I might need them someday. I refused to part with sentimental items that I treated as precious, perhaps even more than the actual events they represented.

Keeping all of this stuff, I believe, was my way of holding onto things that had meaning in my life, because I had been too emotionally frozen to actually enjoy them when they happened. Reliving them was my way of trying to capture something I had let slip through my fingers.

Another huge area that was broken in my life was my faith. I had pursued God so desperately in my early years, all the while convinced that He was mad at me. I believed that all the bad things that happened in my life were His punishment for something terrible that I must have done.

Although my children all received the sacraments, we were not a church-going family. I had been a closet Bible reader as a child, but I did not comprehend the meaning. I just enjoyed the exciting stories of the parting of the Red Sea, Jonah and the whale, and how God stopped Abraham from killing Isaac. These stories were far more enthralling than the books I read voraciously at the library, although I understood those.

There was *Harriet the Spy*, who went on great adventures, and *Nancy Drew*, who could solve anything. *Black Beauty* tugged at my heartstrings, especially when they found him downcast and abused, but there was always *Lassie*, who could save the day and had a home she always wanted to return to.

The Bible, by contrast, was filled with confusing paradoxes—to gain your life, you must lose it; strength is made perfect in weakness;

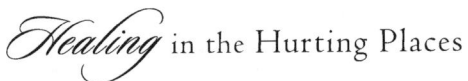 in the Hurting Places

those who are first will become last. I couldn't see that my life was also a confusing paradox.

The final break came when we took our Girl Scout troop to Italy for 14 days—a trip they fully fundraised. As we stood for hours in line waiting to get into the Vatican, we passed beggars and homeless people lying on the streets, asking for food. When we finally entered St. Peter's Cathedral, I found it dripping with gold. It turned my stomach.

Surely this is not how Jesus would have wanted it.

I kept thinking about Jesus' rage in the temple when He threw the moneychangers out and how He preached about the poor. If all the gold was melted down, it would feed all of those hungry people for miles around, I surmised.

I didn't understand how God or Jesus would allow this. I didn't understand how He would allow a child to be repeatedly raped. I left the Catholic Church after that trip and abandoned my faith altogether.

As far as I was concerned, God and the Church had failed the people of Rome and They had failed me. There was no room in my life for failure.

Chapter 3

The Façade Crumbles

It had been a routine workday; everything had run smoothly. I was closing out the books and getting the next day's work laid out. My boss came up to my desk to drop off a file and mumbled something to me as he headed out to run a quick errand before locking up.

I don't recall exactly what he said, but the words he used triggered a memory locked deep inside me. Suddenly, inexplicably, I picked up the tape dispenser—the type with a weighted base—and hurled it through the sliding glass partition in front of my desk.

I'd always had lousy aim, and this was no exception. The dispenser smashed into the closed portion of the partition. I sat in stunned silence as the fragments of glass rained down on my desk and the office floor.

My silence, like the glass…had just been shattered.

I have learned a lot about the devastating effects of childhood sexual abuse since that time. But as I traveled the journey, I took a lot of baby steps that were foreign to me.

Healing in the Hurting Places

Some people might say that I was "lucky," but I know now that I was blessed to have God walk this journey with me even though I didn't recognize His hand on the situation in the beginning. And because of that, He put many people into my life—people who could be "Jesus with skin on"—to help me along the way.

My boss, who is Jewish, was used by God that day to minister to me. Instead of firing me, he recognized the emotional pain I was in; he realized my pain had to be deep to unleash such explosive rage. He handed me a business card for a psychiatrist he knew and urged me to seek help.

I have learned that it matters not what denomination you are, what church you attend, or even if you believe that God exists. God can and will use anyone to accomplish His purposes and bring Him glory, according to His will.

I'd love to say that seeing a psychiatrist was the answer, that I began treatment and was healed. I know that, for many, such treatment has been the turning point. I encourage you to seek out a competent counselor who can listen and guide you. I tried a few and, while each proved helpful in their own way, it was only a small part of the plan that God had in mind for me. The road ahead held lots of twists and turns, and I had just rounded the first bend.

That initial burst of rage opened a new door for me. While I remembered the abuse, I had pushed it down deep inside me. I thought that moving on was part of the way to get past something.

But I now believe that we can truly move on only when we have taken that last walk with God through the experience, no matter how many times we may have relived it on our own. We need to surrender all of our pain, anxiety, and fear to the One who can take it and mold

The Façade Crumbles

it into our good and His glory. Until that point, we will remain stuck in the healing process.

Our precious Savior understands and wants us to walk in the freedom He purchased for us on the cross. The irony is that, in those days, I didn't realize how imprisoned I still was. I had a loving and supportive husband and three beautiful children whom I adored. I had reentered the work force and was poised to climb the corporate ladder. I seemingly had it all—the happy American family, a house with a pool, a responsible job.

I'm sure that until the day I launched the tape dispenser, those who knew me through work, social activities, or the gym I worked out in, considered me your average, normal, well-adjusted person. I worked hard to keep up that appearance. Sadly, it was all an illusion.

It is likely that many people you encounter each day harbor deep secrets that leave them feeling dirty, alone, and ashamed. So they wear masks, just like I did.

Some of them might not even realize they are wearing masks.

Chad (not his real name) was one of those people. I met him at a support group. He was a successful CEO and a newlywed. He thought he was living the American dream until, one day, the vivid childhood memory of being assaulted by his older brother came flooding back.

Suddenly, Chad's life crumbled. He could neither get up in the morning nor be functional. Things were so bad he had to take a leave of absence from his job. He became unresponsive to his wife, who in turn wondered what had become of the man she married.

Chad wanted to believe that the nightmares he'd begun to relive each night were illusions and his once successful, carefree life was reality. So he confronted his brother, hoping to discover that he was

Healing in the Hurting Places

simply losing his mind. Sadly, his brother not only confirmed his awakening memories, but laughed them off as normal, childhood experimentation.

The night I broke the glass was when the nightmares began for me. Detailed memories came racing back, piece by piece. This went on for weeks; soon weeks turned into months. I didn't understand why this was happening.

But at least I knew about my past; I had just buried the details. Chad's mind had repressed them. God has given our minds the amazing ability to repress traumatic events that are too painful to process until such time as we are better equipped to deal with them.

If you ask the victims of a bad automobile accident what happened, most will not be able to recall the details of the impact or the moments leading right up to it. I've attended to people in serious motor vehicle accidents involving severe bleeding or trauma who indicate that they are not in any pain. We call this condition "shock." In a similar way, this is what happens when we are subjected to severe emotional trauma.

Depending on the age and maturity level of the victim at the time of occurrence, the horrific details may simply be too overwhelming to process. So the memories are "stored" in the subconscious until such time as the victim is in a better position to handle them.

This repression is not limited to sexual abuse victims and those injured in auto accidents. There are plenty of documented cases of veterans returning from war and experiencing "flashbacks." Any trauma that is too much for the mind to process can set up what therapists now term *post-traumatic stress syndrome* (PTSS) or *post-traumatic stress disorder*.

Symptoms vary widely, but often include flashbacks of the original event, nightmares, uncontrollable or inappropriate fear, withdrawal, and guilt. Having some or all of these symptoms after a horrific event is normal; it is called *acute traumatic stress syndrome.*

We have been programmed by God for the fight-or-flight response; when the terror diminishes or disappears, our bodies take some time to wind down from our heightened state of arousal and preparedness. However, when these symptoms continue for extended periods of time or leave their victims incapacitated to some degree, PTSS is likely the culprit.

For victims, it is important to know and understand why your body is reacting the way that it is. Often, something called a *trigger* initiates the symptoms. In my case, something that my boss said triggered a distant memory that unleashed the stored-up anger inside. It could be the words someone uses, the tone of voice, a scent, a sound, even something visual. Anything that reminds the victim of a past memory can cause him or her to overreact.

I personally did not experience much of this direct-connection type of trigger. For me, it was more the actions or attitudes of those around me. For example, because I was not believed as a child, someone doubting my word as an adult could bring about a reaction in me.

Triggers are specific to the victim's experiences. Some child victims were locked in closets or made to sleep with the lights off. As adults, they might tend to hyperventilate when entering walk-in closets or when someone turns off the lights at night.

My triggers are also vaguer in this area. Because I was trapped and held against my will, a person blocking the only exit in the room could cause me to react. In the actual abuse memory, there was close physical contact, while in the later scenarios, the person might be standing a few feet from me. It became more about the re-creation of the feeling than the reenactment of an exact situation.

Healing in the Hurting Places

It was enough just to *feel like* I was trapped. At those moments, it was like I was no longer in control and my emotions took over. I would often become vocal, whether that meant yelling, talking fast, speaking irrationally, or crying. I would also try to get out of the situation physically, whether by pushing my way out, distracting the person so I could escape, or even throwing something out of rage.

I can look back now and see what my typical reactions had in common—I was doing as an adult what I hadn't done when I was younger. I often beat myself up mentally for not crying out, pushing away, resisting more forcefully, or screaming. It almost felt like I was trying to make up for what I couldn't do at the time of the abuse. Of course, applying the actions revealed by hindsight to new and different situations resolved nothing.

In fact, the opposite was true. My reactions, just like that day in the office, were red flags to everyone around me that I wasn't the person they had believed me to be. While everyone gets upset or loses their temper from time to time, my irrational actions were letting everyone know that something was very wrong in my world. At the time, I had no idea how obvious my actions were or what message they were sending. All I could do was react.

Afterward, when I saw the startled reactions of onlookers or sensed that I had stepped over the line, I would do some fast backpedaling. These follow-up actions only compounded the problem. I might make illogical excuses for what happened, deny that the behavior even occurred, or in many cases, blame the other party for causing it. *After all, if they hadn't threatened my well-being by standing in the doorway, there would have been no need to react that way*; or so I told myself.

To make matters worse, I had an incredible memory. What I lacked at that point in emotional stability at times, I more than made up for with a memory for the littlest details. I could not only recall a conversation and what was said, but what date it was said on, where it took place, and possibly even what the person was wearing or what the weather was like. My mind would recall details as if seeing them in a picture in my mind.

It was very important for me to remember these details; often, after leaving the place where the event had occurred, I would replay the scene over and over again in my mind, as if to record it. Dialogue was especially important to me. Strangely enough, all of this was very comforting to me.

I liked being able to recall exactly what someone had said to me three years earlier on a particular day. I thought this showed that I was genuinely interested in them and they were important to me. It was only much later that a friend finally convinced me that this behavior was very unnerving to people. She pointed out that she couldn't even remember saying some of this stuff to me, let alone have me quote it back verbatim.

The problem came in when I was triggered and tried to justify my behavior after the fact. If I was blaming someone for what happened, I would often reach into my memory banks and recall some incident that happened years earlier that gave me "cause" for acting this way. I can look back now and see how I was making things worse by doing this.

Manipulating became a crutch for me. I grew up in a very manipulative household, so this was the last behavior I ever wanted to embrace. During my formative years, the behavior I witnessed was very blatant but my manipulative behavior was often subtle and typically involved bringing something up from the past and tying it to the current behavior.

For example, to win an argument, I might remind the person that they said "such-and-such" previously and that's why I acted the way

Healing in the Hurting Places

that I did; I was simply acting on the basis of their earlier suggestion or permission. There are several inherent problems with this, as I came to find out. One: The person probably didn't remember saying what I was quoting. Two: People change their thoughts over time so they might not feel that way any longer. And most importantly, no one wants their words used against them.

There were many years of heartbreak, arguments, and damaged relationships left in my wake due to these behaviors. I know part of the reason I acted inappropriately was because I kept myself isolated growing up and did not have the interaction with peers and others that would have refined my behavior. Some of my childishness would have been addressed by peers or teachers growing up, if I had exhibited it then. I also can't discount the possibility that because I was forced to grow up too fast, I was now acting in the way that I would have more naturally gotten out of my system back then. It's like it was stored up over time and, as my wound was torn open, everything that was never expressed was now being vented.

In some ways, I thought the memories I collected served as artillery to protect me from future attacks. It was an off-kilter defense system. And in an even sadder truth, I think when my actions produced negative results in people and they backed off, I felt safer and more secure. You can't be hurt by someone who is not in your life, and if people were going to leave or back away, better that I took the reins and made it happen. I think it was a means of exerting control.

So many behaviors spring from improper reactions to abuse. For example, because my trust was violated, it was difficult for me to trust others. At the time I was sexually violated, I felt only repulsion and fear; but because God has designed our bodies for sexual intimacy and fulfillment (in a covenant relationship), they can react with pleasure to being touched, even when the relationship is inappropriate. This betrayal by the physical body can lead to punishment of the body, through cutting, promiscuity, anorexia, bulimia, or suicide.

It is not easy to share all of this, but because God has redeemed so much in my life, I can look back and rejoice that I am not that person anymore. As I started to read books on abuse and attend counseling sessions, I discovered that my behavior was actually "normal" for what I went through, as I saw when other sexual abuse victims shared the same unusual behaviors and patterns.

Generally, it seems that the reactions veer in one of two extremes with "society-accepted normalcy" lying in the middle. For example, a young woman may become promiscuous with men because she feels unloved, so she looks for what she considers love in all of the wrong places. Another may become celibate or a lesbian, out of disdain for men, out of fear, or because she feels more comfortable with her own gender.

In my case, I pushed myself to excel—in work, school, and social activities—to try to rise above it all. I thought if only I was good enough, people would see me as good. Some victims go in the opposite direction and stop caring and striving. They wind up in a bad crowd and often abuse substances in order to numb their minds against the negative feelings they have about themselves.

I know there are lots of people from my past who are no longer part of my life because I thought they would leave anyway when they discovered I was worthless. To avoid their rejection, I drove them away. Now I can only pray that, in God's timing, I may be given the chance to explain and restore those relationships.

So many times, I was so needy and desperate deep down to find and feel the love that I didn't think I deserved, that I choked the life

Healing in the Hurting Places

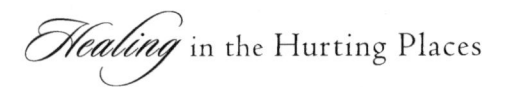

out of those around me. I wanted to believe that they would not give up on me; I outlasted them and wore them down.

In grammar school, I had a wonderful teacher who mentored me in her spare time. I was starved for attention and drank in every drop of the time she offered me. I was so grateful for what she did, but it was not enough to satisfy my pained soul. When she gave attention to another student—someone I didn't like—I flipped out. I wrote her a very long and unpleasant letter, after which she told me that she couldn't help me anymore. In reality, that was an understatement.

The only one who could help me was God. And I was not willing to accept that help for many years.

Chapter 4

Isolation

We have been designed by God to be relational people. In the Book of Genesis, after God created day and night and Heaven and Earth, we read: *"And God saw that it was good"* (Gen. 1:10). This process continued over several days and at the end of the sixth day, Genesis 1:31 tells that *"God saw everything that He had made, and indeed it was very good...."*

Then in chapter two, God suddenly said, *"It is not good that man should be alone; I will make him a helper comparable to him"* (Gen. 2:18). Throughout His Word, we see the relationship that God had with His people and the relationships they had with each other.

In Ecclesiastes, we read:

Two are better than one, because they have a good return for their work: if one falls down, his friend can help him up. But pity the man who falls and has no one to help him up! (Ecclesiastes 4:9-10 NIV)

Jesus assured us that *"Where two or three are gathered together in My Name, I am there in the midst of them"* (Matt. 18:20). This is not at all to say

Healing in the Hurting Places

that Jesus is not with us when we are alone or that He will not hear us unless we are in the presence of others. Rather, it is to teach us the importance of the Body of Christ—how we can lift each other up, hold each other accountable, and gather together in prayer and praise of the One who knew it was not good to be alone.

I recall my first day of high school. I traveled with some of my grammar school companions on the bus ride over. Once we entered the building, we were directed to find our names on a list that would indicate our homeroom classes for our freshman year. I did not recognize any names on the list for my homeroom. It was a relief. I was ready for a fresh start.

I sat down in the assigned area for my class, among the empty seats. Only a few minutes had passed when a ponytailed dirty blonde with freckles approached and introduced herself. Strangely, I did not pull away. I sensed something in her…pain…hurt?

Nothing she said supported that, but I found myself dropping my guard ever so slightly around her. Months of idle chatter amid the day-in, day-out whirlwind of high school ensued until the day she made a casual comment that cracked my veneer. I realized that she had a "different" childhood, although it was also different from mine. Her demons were not the same as mine, but they disturbed her sense of peace just as mine did.

It would be the first time I realized that I could recognize someone else in pain. Something in me cried out with a deep compassion and a desire to heal. I didn't know how to be kind or gentle to myself, but my aching heart was willing to heap tons of compassion on anyone else whose soul cried out to me.

Over time, this unquenchable need to heal and fix others stretched to great lengths. Sick? Driving homemade chicken noodle soup halfway across the state was a no-brainer for me. Depressed? I'd drop everything not only to listen, but I'd take the person out to their favorite place, treat them to food I couldn't afford, and make sure that somehow, I would get a smile on their face. The looks I got in return were bemused, alright—they thought I was crazy!

I saw it as an extension of my do-gooder, excel-to-all-extremes attitude. I didn't realize that what I was really doing was tossing an emotional boomerang, hoping that goodwill and love would be heaped back on me. If I couldn't feel better, well then, I'd just have to make everyone else on the planet well. Then, maybe, just maybe, that would make me feel better.

The irony is that, on the outside, I did feel better. I was happy to be taking an active role in *doing* something. Again, it was all about power and I was wielding control in the situation. But, over time, when reciprocation didn't come—as in the hurting person cheering me up when I felt down—I felt betrayed and stupid for caring.

It became a manipulation game. While I did start out with good intentions for the person in pain; underneath, I was trying to buy love or attention, just like the promiscuous victims were doing. Instead of using my body, I was playing on people's emotions—and getting more hurt in the process.

I have seen this manifest itself over and over again in others. One sexual abuse victim told me she was so hard on others and difficult to be around that she went through two marriages and burned out three business partners. She had revolving door friendships because as she put it, "No one could handle being around me for long periods of time."

Support groups will tell you: "Hurt people hurt people." It is a great paradox that the people who least want to hurt someone else—knowing how it feels—wind up hurting people more than others do. Those who have been hurt act out of a place of pain. They transfer their emotions to those around them. Sometimes this is positive, helping others for example. Other times, it is damaging; they may take their uncontrollable rage out on others because they haven't come to terms with the anger in their own lives.

These wounded behaviors have a domino effect. A sexual abuse victim who becomes an alcoholic may end up marrying or living with "enablers" who cover up inappropriate behaviors instead of confronting them and forcing the alcoholic to get help. While this may be done out of love, and although the enabler truly believes he or she is helping, not realizing the impact of enabling actions only further entrenches the alcoholic behavior (because there are no consequences).

If I acted childishly (if I were a child), I would have been given a time-out or punished in some way. It would, hopefully, have been made clear to me that such behavior was unacceptable and would not be tolerated. This would have taught me that what I was doing was wrong.

But because a lot of this childish behavior did not come out until I was an adult, no one was going to sit me down in a corner or take away my dessert. More than that, no one was going to talk to me after some reflective time had passed in solitude to let me know that my actions needed to change. I often got the solitude—but not the talk. People generally did one of three things: they enabled me, allowing the behavior to become more entrenched; they tolerated me, by ignoring my actions and not holding me accountable; or they left me, which caused the issues to escalate.

Age-inappropriate behavior in high school (or any behavior that doesn't fit the current norm of the school) serves to make the "odd one out" a target. So, during my high school years, already fraught

Isolation

with puberty and awkwardness, my wounded body and soul became further victimized: I was bullied.

Teenagers feeling insecure in their own skin often shore up their self-images by dragging down others. This is why bullying is rampant in this age group.

I already hated myself and everything about me; having others voice the same opinion fostered a desperation that rocked my soul. *What was the point of even being here?*

And so the suicide attempts began.

Some therapists will tell you that suicide attempts are merely a cry for help. The problem can run deeper than that. Sometimes the person has already given up and help is not even a remote possibility in their mind. But for me, it was not at that point yet; I truly was crying out for help. I can look back and know that my attempts were halfhearted; most of them were not serious enough to kill me, but they were certainly strong enough to let people know I was in trouble.

One night, I felt suicidal while on a high school retreat. We had done a lot of soul-searching over the previous two days and my soul contained too much pain to contemplate. The more I thought about it and analyzed it, the more I wanted out. I did tell a few casual friends who, in hindsight, truly cared but didn't know what to do. They told a clergyman and brought me to see him. He told me to go back to my room, say a prayer, and I'd feel better. He told me we all feel like quitting at times.

I have to think that he did not have any training or education in this area because, had I been more serious, it would have been over for me that day. I can't understand why he never made an attempt to find out what was wrong, engage me in conversation, or even have someone

Healing in the Hurting Places

keep an eye on me. I was probably in and out of his office in less than five minutes.

My friends were baffled, too. They stayed up all night in shifts, making sure that I was never alone and always watching me. They didn't question me, either, or talk or pray with me. I'm sure that I probably scared them half out of their minds and they didn't know how to handle me. I give them credit for not abandoning me that night. They kept in touch with me after that, until I married and became someone else's problem.

I have tried to track them down and explain and let them know that God has brought me out on the other side, but the two I was able to locate didn't know what to say. I think learning the truth about why I acted and felt that way was more disturbing to them than the unknown issues had been at the time of the crisis.

As I started to open up to people during my later healing process, I found that unless the person had been abused themselves, they didn't know what to say. *What can you say to someone who was wounded so deeply as a child?* If someone had said to me, "I understand," and they had not gone through the same pain, I would not have been able to believe them. It's akin to telling a cancer patient that you know how they feel when you've never had cancer.

Anger is a very common reaction when people hear what happened to a sexual abuse victim. But this doesn't serve victims well, either. They either have not yet come to terms with the anger inside or they are past that point. Having someone else express an emotion that means nothing to them doesn't bridge the gap, either.

When people wonder why God has allowed abuse in their lives (as I did for a long time) I now believe it is so they can be the ones who

Isolation

do understand other hurting hearts. The ones who can say, "I know how you feel" —and do.

Because abandonment, betrayal, and rejection are common themes in a victim's life, there was a time when what I wanted to hear most was: "I am here for you. I will always be here for you. I am not going anywhere." If someone said that to me, I had trouble believing it because of how I saw myself, but inwardly, I would desperately hope it would turn out to be true.

I did hear those words on a few occasions. And I am very blessed by the people who were able to keep that commitment. But the reality is, people will always—even the ones who stay—disappoint you in some way. *"As it is written: 'There is no one righteous, not even one'...for all have sinned and fall short of the glory of God"* (Rom. 3:10,23 NIV).

Chapter 5

Victim Mentality

Further abuse continued to dog me for many years. When you have a "victim mentality," your persona tends to attract more abuse. It is like two puzzle pieces seeking the right fit: The abuser looks for certain personality traits that he or she can take advantage of and the abused person has already adopted those traits as a result of the original abuse.

For example, I didn't like myself and constantly beat myself up emotionally. I believed that no one else liked me either or wanted to be around me. This made me a prime target for someone to come alongside and contradict those messages—someone who could lavish attention and encouragement on me. I was so parched emotionally that everything in me screamed for this, although I didn't see it at the time. I believed that I did a good job of hiding things, which, to a degree, was true for many years.

But just as the abused can often recognize other abuse victims by their behavior, abusers also have this fine-tuning. For example, pedophiles engage in actions called "priming"; this is simply a process of

Healing in the Hurting Places

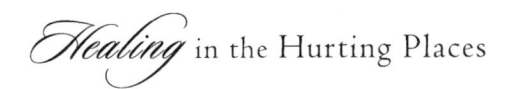

breaking down barriers that a victim has put up so the pedophile can gain the target's trust.

No one wants to be abused. And when the pattern starts up again, some strange dynamics occur. One, the person being abused feels horribly victimized again. All of the negative feelings from the original abuse are multiplied. But, in a strange sort of way, it also feels comfortable, because it has become the victim's reality; it is what he or she knows. We are all creatures of habit. Familiar surroundings, no matter how horrible, will always feel like home to us.

Victims already understand the role; sadly, it fits like a glove, because they have become conditioned to act in certain ways. Perhaps a woman is being abused by her husband. She learns to avoid the triggers that provoke his anger. The problem is that the original problem is never addressed. Therefore, new behaviors will become triggers, because the behavior isn't actually what's causing the problem. The issue runs much deeper than that.

This is why so many children of alcoholics grow up and marry alcoholics, sometimes more than once. I know of women who have entered into second and third marriages—all with alcoholics. A few dynamics are at work here. The child of an alcoholic will probably grow up too fast. If a parent is too drunk to prepare dinner or clean the house, the child will often step into these roles. He or she will become an enabler, providing a means for the alcoholic to continue in their dependency while others handle the world around them.

The logical order of the parent taking care of the child is reversed. Suddenly, it is the child taking care of the parent. Deep down, the child may resent the loss of childhood and the normal, child-appropriate freedom from adult responsibilities. Outwardly, however, the child steps up to the plate and performs. Their personality adapts to

Victim Mentality

the caregiver role and when the child becomes an adult, he or she often subconsciously seeks out someone who needs "tending to."

People raised in such environments will clean up the vomit and throw out the empty bottles as though on autopilot. It is familiar to them and, in a way, it brings them comfort because it is something they know how to do well. Their inebriated parent may never have given them positive messages; or the children may not have been willing to believe their inebriated parents, having witnessed the many lies and excuses common to alcoholics. But being able to turn childhood chaos into something they could control helped them to survive their environments—so now they seek it out.

I heard the heartbreaking testimony of a woman who had been abused for years by her husband. She had been beaten to within inches of her life many times, but she stayed in the marriage for the same reasons that many abused women do: she said she loved him. Perhaps she did in her own way. But I think she also loved the fact that he stayed with her.

Victims believe that no one wants them or loves them and that is why they have been abused. They believe they asked for it, they deserved it, and once others find out what they are really like, they will leave. On some level, this is what victims feel in their hearts. Then they grow up and marry people who shoot down this belief and stay with them, no matter what. The victims can't leave on their own, because to do so would mean rejecting the one person who stood up to their negative thoughts and disproved them. They want to believe in their hearts that these negative tapes they have played over and over again in their own heads are not true. And their abusers hold the key to that.

Over time, this woman was thrown down staircases, had most of her bones broken, and still she stayed. Another reason that this pattern continues is because victims feel that they have no other options. The

Healing in the Hurting Places

abuser may control the money in the house. They may have been possessive and cut the victims off from friends and family and possibly a job outside the home, so they believe that they have no resources for an exit.

They may also feel that their abusers not only love them, but need them. They remember back to the days of taking care of their needy parent—if they left, what would happen to the abuser? Just as a parent bears responsibility for taking care of a child, when the roles are reversed, the child feels an obligation that must be fulfilled.

This continues on in the new abusive relationship. So the victim can't leave; doing so would mean being a "bad person" for shirking responsibility. Again, there is a need for victims to feel like they are "good" while, internally, their mental tapes are telling them they are bad. These opposite messages collide with each other over and over again.

Everyone has their breaking point and hopefully—eventually—realizes the need to escape. There are many resources today where women and men can get the help they need to exit dangerous situations safely.

The woman I just mentioned is a volunteer with one of those organizations. On the day I heard her speak, she was talking to teenagers, teaching them to recognize the warning signs of dangerous relationships when dating. She went on to say that when she reached her breaking point and tried to get out, her husband discovered her leaving. He loaded his gun and shot her as she ran from the house.

Wounded and bleeding, she stopped. She hesitated, turned, and went back to him. For those who have never been in an abusive situation, that action might seem insane. You might be wondering what she was thinking. Or if you have healed from such a situation, your heart goes out to her because you do understand.

As she told her story that day, I understood, too. She was not only shot that day, but the myth she wanted to believe was also shot down. If her husband truly loved her, if she really was worth something, if she deserved to live, then why was he trying to take that from her?

When it comes to breaking points, it matters not that the abuser has come close to that point many times before. Close doesn't count because victims develop a high level of tolerance for emotional pain. It has to reach the point where something inside them snaps, a point at which the abuser's behavior finally crosses a bar that is too high even for them.

Being shot had not yet brought this woman to her breaking point. The victim mentality clouds reality; the victim often deduces the following: *If my abuser doesn't love me the way I thought he (or she) did, then I am the piece of garbage I have been told I was. There is nothing left for me other than the life I know. Getting out of the situation now serves no purpose, because there is nothing positive to move toward.*

Once hopelessness has set in, it doesn't matter how good the next situation looks; the victim has learned to see it as a lie. He or she surmises that the final outcome could be worse than the current mayhem. It's the old story of the devil you know being better than the one you don't.

The woman volunteer continued her testimony and explained that, as she turned to head back to her husband, he shot her again.

Through the grace of God, the innate part that He gave each of us in order to survive, reared its head in that moment, despite the years of her emotional and physical pain. Finally, she chose to value her "worthless self" over the lies of the devil. She turned away from

Healing in the Hurting Places

her husband and God gave her the strength to physically walk out of that situation and into a new life—one that shattered those old lies and myths.

The emotional strength came much later and multiplied each time she took another victim under her wing and sat next to their hospital bed, or on the bench in the courthouse as they awaited their divorce or custody hearings. I watched her strength increase as she spoke to the girls in the room that night, hoping to encourage them to make the right choices and avoid what she went through.

This victim mentality doesn't only attract more abuse and keep the victim hostage to satan's lies; it also breaks the victim down in another paradox. On the outside, I presented this tough, capable, independent exterior. But on the inside, I was weak, scared, and beaten down. My spirit was broken in a lot of ways.

This was another reason I was afraid to let anyone get too close to me. It went beyond the fear of being hurt again or of having my hopes raised, only to have them dashed. I was also afraid that people would see that I was an imposter.

To protect my false image, I strove and pushed and excelled. I wanted people to notice all of the good I was doing, so they wouldn't stop to look and see the *real* me. Basically, I created a smoke screen.

What I didn't realize was this: All of that *trying* made me look out of place. If I had only lessened my efforts, I might have blended in better. Instead, I became a giant red flag to everyone because my behavior was out of the ordinary for any situation I was put in. If a group was looking for a volunteer, I was first in line. But I didn't just donate my time; I purchased supplies, worked at it every chance I had, and went overboard on the whole project.

Victim Mentality

I often second-guessed myself when I was tasked with buying something. Instead of making a decision on a particular item, I would find myself paralyzed and unable to decide. Rather than come back empty-handed, I'd buy all of the available options. When I returned, laden with packages, the recipient's eyes would widen. Yet, I never took the hint. Instead, I beamed with delight that I had overwhelmed them with my enthusiasm.

It's only now that I can look back and see how sad and pathetic I must have looked. I did the most bizarre things for people. If it was someone I cared about, I moved Heaven and Earth to let them know I cared. When a transit strike prevented me from taking mass transportation to meet a date, I set out early and walked for miles—even across a bridge—to show him that nothing was going to stop me. That should have told me something about how out of control I was. Instead, it just fed me more.

As I mentioned earlier, when someone was sick, I dropped everything to make and deliver homemade chicken soup—even to the other side of the state. I didn't buy cooked chicken pieces or stock; I bought a whole chicken, slow-cooked it, and made my own stock from scratch.

If someone suggested that they liked or needed something, it was the equivalent of a pistol going off in my head to start a race. I would hunt down the desired item, get it to them posthaste, and then wait for the reaction. The honest reaction was almost always shock and surprise, but I twisted that in my head to think that they were shocked to learn that I cared about them that much.

If I surprised someone with a homemade lunch, I made menus to go along with it, as if they were in a fancy restaurant. I remember during one of my really low periods, I even went to the dry goods store and purchased material in their favorite color and whipped up a tablecloth to go along with the homemade meal.

Healing in the Hurting Places

I know now how bizarre these actions sound. When I was called out on this behavior, I became defensive because I was doing something "good." *Couldn't they see that? It had to be their issue; maybe they never had someone treat them that nicely before,* I thought.

Internally, I cringed. *Once again, I'm being misunderstood; I can't win no matter what. Bad things happen to me because I must be bad. Now I am doing something good, something more than other people do, and it is still being looked at the wrong way.*

No matter how much I pushed or took things to extremes, it was still not enough. I would wonder: *What is it going to take to get them to see that I am not bad? Or is there no good inside me at all for them to see?* These thoughts haunted me.

When I attended a group for other sexual abuse survivors, we all exchanged similar battle stories. I have also heard these above-and-beyond tales from children of alcoholics and drug addicts. It is about people pleasing to the umpteenth degree.

It was then that God started to open my eyes and help me see that my motivations were not purely altruistic. They were more of a boomerang effect. Deep down, I was giving to these people what I so desperately wanted: love and attention. I went to all lengths because I was so needy and lacking.

When He revealed that to me, I broke down in tears. I really and truly wanted with all of my heart to believe that I had the purest of motivations. Now that I can see things clearer, I can realize and appreciate that I did really have a heart to do something nice for the people I cared about. It was my own hurt that took positive actions and ran with them.

I believe I actually fed off of the good feelings I was projecting toward the people I gave to. My world was so negative that I tried to create good things all around me as a counterbalance. On some level, I was turning the giving around in my head: What I wanted to receive, I gave instead. It was an attempt, albeit subconsciously, to satisfy a need down deep inside.

I also learned that people who have had difficult or sad childhoods, look for the happy ending. At all costs, I wanted the happy ending. I know as a child, people saw how different I was. I didn't know it then, but I've been told this as an adult by those who knew me when I was little. They saw how standoffish I was and how I preferred the company of older adults to kids my own age.

What I remember is a strong dislike to anything that appealed to my age group. For example, I hated circuses. And parades. And Walt Disney movies—the comedies. The sad ones like *Old Yeller* and *The Three Lives of Tomasina*, I would watch over and over again. On the inside, I cried for the hurting characters. It mattered not that I knew they weren't real. On the outside, I would stoically watch the movie over and over again, until I could recite the lines by heart. In a way, this may have been the training ground for memorizing all of the details that would become my signature later in life.

I hated books that started with "Once upon a time" because the endings were always syrupy, like the ordinary girl winds up with a prince and lives happily ever after. But the reason those stories appeal to children is because there is a part of us that yearns for peace and tranquility. We all want the happy ending in life.

As an adult, I very much wanted all of the negative stories in my life to end that way. Even if it meant forcing the ending....

Chapter 6

The Cycle Continues

It is not difficult to see why I became an easy mark when I got to high school. I was friendly...too friendly. I hung out with a group of homeroom girls who shared other classes with me. I attended an all-girls, private, Catholic high school where the uniform consisted of gray skirts, blue boleros, and starched white shirts. The student body may have looked wholesome and innocent, but the opposite was true for most. About three-quarters of the girls smoked, drank, and got high on a regular basis. At least ten percent of my class admitted to having abortions before the age of 18.

But the girls I associated with joined guitar clubs, took drama, or worked on the school newspaper and yearbook. They excelled in school and stayed out of trouble. They say that there is safety in numbers, but even in that group, I seemed "different" and quickly became a mark.

Just like in the wild, predators quickly eye the weaker among them. The rest of the group then surges forth in self-defense, leaving the

Healing in the Hurting Places

weaker one alone to fend for itself. Nature calls this "survival of the fittest"; I call it a tough way to get through high school.

It started out small with name-calling and remarks made loud enough to hear as I walked by. It quickly snowballed into notes and messages taped to my locker. One day, I walked into religion class and heard the now familiar snickering. As I took my seat without looking up, the laughter grew louder. I slowly raised my head and saw my name chalked on the blackboard along with a derogatory message.

I fought to hold back the tears, but it really wasn't necessary. I had pushed them so far down inside me that I wouldn't have been able to coax them out if I'd tried. I ignored the stares and pretended I was someplace else. I was skilled at this; I survived the abuse by distancing my mind from what was taking place.

I'd be lying if I said the vile message didn't cut me to the quick. I couldn't ignore the irony of this happening in a religion class, of all places. Then, out of the corner of my eye, I saw two girls I had been friends with in grammar school walk up to the blackboard, pick up the erasers, and boldly wipe away the disgusting words. I have never forgotten their act of bravery, because siding with me meant opening themselves up to the same ridicule I had endured. This is why, little by little, the group of girls I originally hung with drifted away. Fewer than ten friends remained at my side by the time we graduated.

For some unknown reason, these two girls were not tortured for their courage. I can only assume that God protected them. I've often wished I had an ounce of their courage. I doubt that I or most of us would have done the same thing in their place. High school girls can be cruel and no one wants to stand out during the turbulent teenage years.

The administration was aware of the bullying; in fact they blamed me for causing the problems in school. In researching the bullying effect in school systems, I have learned that this is not uncommon. It is easier to point the finger of blame at what appears to be the origin of the problem, than to dig deeper and discover the cause.

Also, sadly, in a lot of these cases, bullying is done by those who have been permitted to get away with it for many reasons.[1] Their actions have never had consequences and people have looked the other way. It didn't help that my family wasn't donating library wings to the school or wasn't politically connected, like the families of my adversaries.

One day, I walked into the cafeteria for lunch. A meatball sailed through the air as I entered and found its mark on my gray skirt. Laughter ensued. Then another meatball landed, and another. As I turned to leave, someone dumped a plate of spaghetti on my head. The volunteers serving the food stood by and said nothing.

With my white blouse stained in marinara sauce and strands of pasta clinging to my hair, I went into the bathroom to address the damage.

Some of the girls followed me in, laughing and pointing. I walked out and into the main office to explain the situation and get a pass so I could change and wear my "street clothes" for the remainder of the day. The principal called me into her office and surveyed the damage. She told me sternly that I must have done something to provoke this attack and said, "Now you must wear your consequences."

She refused to give me the pass.

The laughter and stares followed me from room to room as I got through the rest of the day's classes. I can honestly say that, as embarrassing as it was, I had almost become numb to what was going on. I had to, in order to come back each day and endure more.

Healing in the Hurting Places

One day, I was pushed down the stairs of the bus as I was getting ready to exit. I landed in the street and as the bus pulled away I could hear the girls chanting their taunts out the window.

Several times I was locked in classrooms while the girls made faces and held signs up to the glass window in the door.

Early on, I got fed up and decided to confront some of the girls. I asked them, "Why are you doing this to me? I am a person just like you. How would you feel if someone did this to you?" But each question was met with a blank stare and growing snickers. As I turned and walked away, realizing I would never get my answer, they burst into laughter.

When I look back on that day and on how I felt at the time, I see how the roots of my overwhelming and out-of-control gift-giving stemmed from that moment. What I didn't get from those girls—an acknowledgment, an apology, or even a flicker of remorse—I determined would never be withheld by me from anyone I cared about. I would go to any lengths to make sure that they knew that they were loved, appreciated, and cared for. They would never feel alone and outcast.

I think this is why sick people particularly pushed my buttons. My faulty radar told me that something was wrong in the ill person's world and I needed to correct it. Treating the common cold as if it were an all-out attack on the person's character was the equivalent of putting a plaster cast on a hangnail. The ailment would have taken care of itself. The "patient" was not seeking a cure and certainly not the Rx I threw at it.

But I didn't look at it this way. The person's attitude mattered most to me; I wanted them to feel better, happy, good about themselves. The look of surprise in response to my efforts was the polar opposite

The Cycle Continues

of my own pained expression as I turned away from the bullying girls in the hall years earlier.

I'm grateful beyond words that over time, God revealed all of this to me. It was as if He held a mirror up to my past and helped me draw parallels between the pain I couldn't express in my youth and the overreactions I expressed later.

Truth be told, the now rational side of me would like to write out these memories once and for all, understand them in all their complexity, and then lock them away in some drawer forever or burn them in some victory bonfire. But as I pour out my soul, God keeps putting people in my path who now encourage me, telling me that this is what they needed to hear, that they know someone who will benefit from my words, or that it has personally ministered to their hearts.

I have to keep reminding myself that if God brought me through all of these circumstances and blessed me with the gift to write about them, then He has a purpose for this that must be fulfilled. It is my heart's desire that He be glorified through this, and so I continue with one last high school story.

These snapshots are just pieces of a bullying saga that lasted four years and even spread to neighboring schools. It was like a flame continually fanned and refusing to be extinguished. While I am not looking to blame anyone, and I have forgiven in my heart those who came against me, I still feel that the administration was accountable for not squelching the problem before it got out of control or taking back control once the matter had spread. Their silence and implied consent (expressed by not taking any action to shut things down) allowed the problem to grow, I believe.

I say this because, sadly, these problems are continuing at an alarming rate in schools across our country. We need to better educate our

Healing in the Hurting Places

counselors, teachers, and administrators in spotting the danger signs before it is too late. It is the reason that I am willing to share some painful parts of my life, in the hopes that it will help others. We do not solve problems by pretending they do not exist.

Unfortunately, I learned that lesson the hard way.

It was early afternoon of testing week and the only students in school were those scheduled for exams that day. All of the faculty members were occupied in classrooms proctoring the tests. I completed my last paper and slipped into a nearby restroom to change into my street clothes. I lived a few miles from school and we passed several public schools on the route home. The public school students loved to pick on the private school kids, so we all changed out of our uniforms to avoid recognition.

I slid the metal bolt across the door, hung the plastic bag with my clothes on the hook, and slipped out of my uniform. I kicked off my shoes, removed my socks, and as I stood there in my underwear, I heard the sound of several girls entering the restroom. Before I could react, hands reached over my stall door and snatched the bag containing my clothes. Other hands simultaneously reached under the door and grabbed my discarded uniform, socks, and shoes.

I heard the clatter of shoes against plastic toilet seats as the ringleaders climbed onto them in the stalls on either side of mine and peered over at me. Apparently satisfied, they got down and, in loud voices, began charging the other girls money to gain admittance to the side stalls to "view" me in my embarrassment and shame.

I felt like a freak in a sideshow. Everything inside of me wanted to scream, *How can you treat me like this? I'm not some animal in a circus. I am a human being. How would you like to be treated like this?*

But my words could find no voice.

The Cycle Continues

The girls continued climbing up, laughing, and pointing. Even though I had my underwear on, I felt exposed and ashamed. I was being mocked, and it hurt. While the sideshow was going on, some of the other girls grabbed wads of paper towels and stuffed them around the perimeter of my stall, igniting them with their lighters before pushing them under. I watched in silence as they covered the border of the stall with their self-made pyres.

Much has been written about "mob mentality" and about how depraved behavior fuels others to act in ways they might not consider if they were alone in similar situations. It becomes easier to "go along with the crowd" than to take a stand against them. This was clearly in play here as more paper was thrown under the stall in an effort by all to participate in this sickening game.

My uncle was a firefighter and all I could think of at that moment was his warning about how most people don't die from the fire themselves, but from smoke inhalation. I thought of how the space under the stall was being closed up by burning piles of paper, forcing the smoke inward and upward. I remember squeezing my eyes shut and saying to myself, *Take me now, God, I'm done. Just take me out of this miserable existence. I can't do this anymore.*

And from that place deep inside me, a familiar refrain rose up: *I will keep you safe.* I knew it was God talking to me, but I didn't understand the message any more than I did when I was being raped and I heard those words for the first time.

How are you keeping me safe? I questioned.

I will keep you safe, He pressed on my heart once more.

As quickly as they came in, the girls left. The fires died out as they consumed the paper piles scattered on the hard, white, tile floor.

Healing in the Hurting Places

Somehow, I found my clothes and dressed and left. I don't remember that part. I do remember visibly shaking for hours and walking all of those miles back home because I was too embarrassed to get on a public bus and have anyone see me in my shame.

I also remember that I never said thank you to God at the time for delivering me from that fiery scenario or for all of the other times that He'd kept me safe. I didn't feel safe at that moment. I strongly wished that I had died, so I would not have to return to school the next day and face my tormentors again.

Years later, when reflecting back on these incidents, I would be comforted with words from the Scripture that reflect God's promise to each of us:

> *To you, O* LORD, *I lift up my soul; in You I trust, O my God. Do not let me be put to shame, nor let my enemies triumph over me. No one whose hope is in You will ever be put to shame, but they will be put to shame who are treacherous without excuse* (Psalm 25:1-3 NIV).

> *The* LORD *Himself goes before you and will be with you; He will never leave you nor forsake you. Do not be afraid; do not be discouraged* (Deuteronomy 31:8 NIV).

ENDNOTE

1. Myths and misperceptions about school bullying, Parents Say Schools Blame Victim, Avoid Bully, Mom: School Protects Bully, Forces Daughter To Move: *Bully Stays In Class With 12-Year Old Victim,* forum,

Chapter 7

Floodwaters

Clu-clunk...clu-clunk...clu-clunk. The wipers struggled to keep up with the deluge. I strained to see through the rain-streaked windshield as I sped up the turnpike. I had listened to the voicemail only minutes earlier: My husband Bill had been rushed to the emergency room. No status was given, but the caller said it might be his heart. Bill's father had died at an early age of a massive heart attack.

I can't lose him, God. He has to be all right, I tried to reassure myself. I had not yet called the kids; I didn't want to alarm them until I knew more. I knew my way around the city without a map, but as I drove out of the tunnel and traversed the familiar neighborhood, I could no longer remember which street the hospital was on.

The worn-out wiper blades made reading signs almost an impossibility. I checked the passenger seat for the street address I had scrawled on a piece of paper before leaving, only to realize it was still on my kitchen table back home. As the traffic light turned red, I gently braked and put my head down on the steering wheel. *God, please help me, I can't find the hospital.*

Healing in the Hurting Places

God and I really didn't have much of a relationship, if any, at the time. I hadn't been to church in years; I figured that He had given up on me a very long time ago. I tried other churches, but I was just going through the motions. I didn't feel anything, so after a while, it didn't make sense to go and pretend.

I'm not sure why I called out to Him that night; I guess for the same reason that they say there are no atheists in foxholes. And when I lifted my head up from the steering wheel, there was the hospital, right across the street. *Had I not stopped for the red light, I would have missed it,* I told myself. In less than three seconds, I had forgotten who delivered me that night.

My husband looked wonderful as I walked in. He was sitting up in bed and his face was flush with color. His vital signs were stable and other than the oxygen provided to ease his breathing, he looked fine. I rode the elevator up to radiology with him and waited while they did a CAT scan.

When they were finished, they wheeled him back into the elevator waiting to take us down to the emergency room. We didn't know about the phone call that the radiologist made as we descended the one flight. When the doors opened, a crash team was waiting to snatch my husband's gurney. I was sent out of the emergency room as they rushed into action.

Bill was diagnosed with a 90 percent blockage in both lungs due to a pulmonary embolism. Often called a silent killer for its hardly noticeable symptoms, it was the third leading cause of instant death in the United States at the time. His heart, straining to overcompensate for the oxygen-depleted blood, had nearly doubled in size.

For the next three weeks, we did not know whether Bill would live or die as the doctors worked to break up the blood clot. If they thinned his blood too quickly, he risked a stroke. But if they did not break it up quickly enough, he was in danger of dying from the effects of the embolism and the strain on his heart. It was a delicate balancing act.

Driving home that first night, I still couldn't find tears. I was a child the last time I cried. My mind raced over the events of the last few months, trying to keep my mind off the present trauma. I had learned the art of taking my mind someplace else so that I didn't have to deal with a reality that was too much to handle. Most abused children learn to master this trick early on.

The reality was overwhelming. The company I worked for had recently been bought out; a grueling training schedule and long hours, along with the school courses I was taking, had finally taken their toll on my own health. Unable to fight off a sinus infection, the bug traveled into my lungs and ears, turning into pneumonia and vertigo. The vertigo made driving impossible; every time I turned my head, everything spun around and I became sick to my stomach. The doctor ordered me out on disability. The new company promptly fired me, in violation of the Family Medical Leave Act.

I didn't have the money to sue and they denied my unemployment claim. The vertigo had begun to subside, but the doctor had not medically cleared me to go back to work. I was without a job and unable to complete my schooling. I had just started a new business and the bills were piling up. Bill had used up his sick and vacation time over a hospitalization the previous year. The only one now working in our household was our oldest child, whose job was downsized the day my husband was rushed to the emergency room.

There was no income, a pile of unpaid bills, and no idea how I was going to keep a roof over our heads and food in the pantry. Yet, it was

Healing in the Hurting Places

up to me to figure it out. I could not bother Bill with this now. I handled the mounting stress like I had always done: in my own strength.

Keeping my focus on what I needed to do to get through each 24-hour period, I plowed ahead, taking each step as it came. I'd had years of practice.

The day that Bill was released, my other daughter was in an auto accident with a tractor trailer that jackknifed, taking down three telephone poles and closing the road for five hours while crews repaired the damage. Her car was totaled; it looked like it had just come out of a compactor. The first police officer responding to the scene didn't believe my daughter was the driver; her sole injury was a friction burn on her inside arm caused when the air bag deployed.

It was months before my husband was able to return to work, and I was still without a job and unemployment insurance. I went through five appeals before my claim was finally approved, almost a year after I was fired. During this time period, I tried to get my own business off the ground. As word of my family's dire straits got out, I landed a few "sympathy jobs." I had set up the company, financials, bookkeeping, and legal paperwork. I was able to do a chunk of the work, but some fell outside my capabilities, so now I needed to hire up.

I felt fortunate to hire someone who appeared talented and capable. More work poured in, and after a year of ups and downs, I felt like I was finally coming out of the drama that had encapsulated my life.

That's when the bottom fell out.

With numerous jobs in the hopper and networking connections being made, things were looking up—until my sole employee quit after stealing money from my company.

That was the fatal blow for me. Until then, I had staggered along, trying not to look at the carnage in my path, because I knew if I stopped to breathe and assess how bad things really were, I wouldn't have the strength to move forward.

But even though I didn't have God in my life at this time, He had me in His....

As I looked at the ocean that night, I thought about God for the first time in months. I really didn't know why I had come to the shore that night; it was as if something called me. I watched the waves pitch and roll and thought back to the many times over the years that I had surveyed this scene and tried to find God in its power and majesty. I believed God created all of it and it took my breath away each time I came to the shore. But He was off in the distance and wanted nothing to do with me.

As a child, I spent hours pressing my knees into the worn red kneeler, fingering my rosary beads as I stared up at the porcelain Jesus hanging lifelessly on His wooden cross. I stared into those eyes and saw nothing but the paint. My soul was as cold as the marble columns surrounding me.

I had asked Jesus over and over to save me, to protect me. I wanted Him to come into my heart when I made my first Holy Communion, but a plain white wafer melted on my tongue instead. I spent so many years trying to figure out why God was mad at me. *What had I done? Why could He not forgive me? Where is He? Why didn't He love me, like the books said He did?*

As I stared into those waves, the same questions from my youth came flooding back. And there weren't any answers this time, either. I started to walk into the water. I planned to keep on walking until I couldn't feel anything any longer. I was so tired of the feelings that

Healing in the Hurting Places

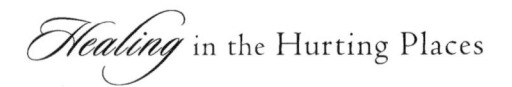

were bottled up inside me. I was tired of trying to be brave, successful, and everything else I thought would make a difference, but hadn't.

There just wasn't any point anymore. I'd held on for over 40 years; now I was so tired, I just wanted it to be over. I couldn't do it anymore. I had always done things in my own strength—and that strength was ebbing out of me just like the waves pulling back from the shore.

I was waist deep in the sea when I heard the faint strumming of a guitar.

When I was four years old, I heard my first guitar song. It was "You'll Know We Are Christians by Our Love." In church, I would sing my heart out as the guitar played.

I didn't recognize what this guitar was playing now, but its sad, sweet melody caught my ears and trickled down into my heart as I turned away from my watery depths.

God had another plan for me that night, and it was just beginning to unfold.

Chapter 8

Streams in the Desert

I followed the strains of guitar music to a ragtag group assembled on the beach, singing to a praise and worship song. I lingered on the outside of the group, drawn, but not sure why.

The music ended and the guitarist began to pray: "I lift up those who are seeking You, whose hearts are broken, but do not know where to find You. Meet them where they are. Touch their hearts and help them to know You, Lord."

I shivered.

I had never heard anyone "free frame" a prayer before. The only prayers I knew were rote ones from my childhood. I felt as if the person leading the prayer knew what was churning up inside my heart, although that was impossible. I looked at the group; all their eyes were closed and their heads bowed. I had expected them to be staring at me, seeing my desolation for what it was.

Healing in the Hurting Places

Whoever these folks were, I wanted nothing to do with them. Standing there made me feel strange inside. I hoped that they hadn't seen me walk over. I left before they could open their eyes.

But as I drove home, I could not get the words of that prayer out of my mind.

A few weeks later, I was idly Web-surfing in my office. I stumbled onto a Website for a church movement that started in California, birthed during the turbulent '60s when so many were seeking for something worthwhile to quench their unrest.

I read about how hippies in torn, dirty jeans, long hair, and bare feet were welcomed into the sanctuary to worship their Lord. This impressed me, as this was always how I envisioned Jesus would have it; after all, He walked among the lepers, tax collectors, and thieves and ministered to all of them. In some churches, this mode of attire would be unacceptable and the youth would have been barred from entering.

Then I read the story of Jon Courson.[1] He was driving with his wife, the love of his life, when a patch of ice on a dark Oregon road caused the car to skid and hit a tree, claiming her life instantly. In the ambulance, he knew she was dead and yet he felt "peace that surpasses all understanding." And he was at peace—not guilt-ridden for having been the driver, not racked with grief over his incredible loss, but silently trusting in God to see him through this crisis. *Oh, to have that kind of faith!*

The curious feelings that had begun welling up in me at the beach that night grew stronger. I wanted to know what it was like to experience this kind of trust in my soul—to possess a "peace that surpasses all understanding" (see Phil. 4:7).

I looked to see if the church had any locations near me and found one about a half hour's drive from my home. I noted the service time and address and considered the possibility of just "checking it out" the following Sunday.

That night, I became very ill. Around 4 a.m., I lay there, doubled over with stomach pains, reviewing what I might have eaten recently to cause this. As I struggled to fall back asleep, the nightmares and flashbacks began. I sat up, my pillow drenched in sweat. I got up and splashed cold water on my face and returned to bed.

By the morning, my head throbbed with a migraine, something I had never had before. I was convinced that it must be food poisoning. But as the day wore on, I became light-headed and dizzy and anxiety clutched at my soul.

That night, the worst moments of my life replayed themselves again as I tossed and turned in the bed. I had heard of people claiming that their life flashed before them just before death; I wondered if I was dying.

Every day, the symptoms multiplied and increased in intensity. The nightmares were relentless. I had started experiencing flashbacks several years earlier, but never to this degree. And I didn't have the physical ailments that I was experiencing now. *Did I have a brain tumor? Had I contracted some horrible disease? Was I losing my mind?*

Sunday dawned and I could barely crawl out of bed in my weakened state. I had planned on checking out the church I read about, but didn't see how I could drive with the way I felt. As I jumped in the shower, I decided there was no way I could make it to the church. But as the water beat down on me, I pictured the lonely waves crashing against the jetty that night at the beach and knew that somehow, I had to try to get to that church.

Healing in the Hurting Places

When I pulled into the parking lot, I became violently ill and thought that this must be satan telling me that I did not belong here. *But would stepping into the church cast my fate toward hell, or free me from the living hell that was each day?* I put my head down on the steering wheel and prayed for God to tell me what to do—should I go in or leave?

"I don't know what to do anymore, God. Please help me," I pleaded.

I found myself walking from the car; it was almost as if I was watching someone else in my body move across the asphalt. I entered the building and my symptoms vanished instantly as I crossed the threshold. I was so stunned that I wanted to step back through the doorway to see if they returned, but the pastor had spotted me and interrupted my confusion. "First time here?" he asked.

That obvious, I thought. *I must have "newbie" stamped on my forehead.*

I managed to nod "yes" and he put out his hand and introduced himself. With a hand on my shoulder, he led me around the church, pointing out where the bathrooms, book room, and sanctuary were. I was so surprised that this busy man was taking time out to show me around the place. I thanked him and quickly ducked into the sanctuary.

Grabbing a Bible from the back, I tried to find the most obscure seat in the place. I opened the bulletin and tried to read, but the words blurred. *Great, am I going to start to need reading glasses?* I wondered. Then I realized, I couldn't read the words because they were moving back and forth. Literally. My hands were shaking.

Everyone stood up as the service began. Guitar music played and the lyrics appeared on a large projection screen. I followed along as more people began to fill in the seats. I was relieved when we could sit down. I looked to the people on either side of me, wondering if they saw how much I was shaking.

As the pastor who welcomed me began his teaching, the tremors subsided. I expected him to talk about some mundane thing, as was the usual custom for the churches I had experienced. I always tried hard to listen to what they had to say, but found myself daydreaming before long. But I hung on every word this pastor had to say; I found him to be a captivating speaker.

That was before he started catching my eye as he looked around the room. And before he started speaking of anxiety and depression—the topic of that day's sermon. *Anxiety and depression? Church topics? And why does it seem that lately, everyone knows what is on my heart? Is it that obvious?*

When he finished speaking, he read a simple prayer stating that you acknowledge that you are a sinner and that Jesus died for your sins and you accept Him as your Savior. As he read those words, I noticed the Bible in my hands began to shake again. But it wasn't just my hands; all of me was quivering in that seat. My palms became sweaty and my heart started to pound.

The pastor asked those who prayed that simple prayer for the first time and meant it to come forward so that they could be welcomed and begin their new lives. I looked at the people sitting on either side of me; their eyes were closed and their heads bowed. They did not see me shaking. I wanted to leave.

But at the same time, I had just heard a new revelation—that Jesus' death on the cross paid the price for my sins once and for all—that there was nothing I could do to earn my way into Heaven, and that all of my striving in life would never get me in.

Healing in the Hurting Places

The pastor then said that if your heart was pounding and your hands were sweaty, it was the Holy Spirit calling your heart. He said that if this was you, to come up as they played another song. For the third time in two weeks, it was as if the speaker knew my heart and could see right through me. I was not used to people seeing through my mask, and it was very unnerving.

The worship leader began. The pastor had looked right at me when he said those words, or at least, it seemed as if he did. He talked about making a decision before it was too late. My mind flashed back to that night on the beach, when, had it not been for the timeliness of the guitar strains, it would have been too late. I thought about how I had wanted Jesus to come into my heart as a little child, but thought He didn't want to. I felt scared, confused...and somewhere deep inside me, a sense of panic. And yet, an incredible invitation had just been extended to me...I had been given another chance.

Please, I prayed, *I don't want it to be too late for me.* I rose from my seat and slowly walked toward the aisle. I felt myself moving forward without any deliberate thought, just as I had done earlier when crossing the parking lot. As I advanced, my eyes were on the back door. I surveyed the crowd—all still had their eyes shut. I could bolt out the door quickly and no one would see me. I gauged whether I had enough time to make my getaway.

The song ended as I found myself at the first row, with a death grip on the end seat. The pastor opened his eyes and waved for me to step forward. I didn't see the pastor anymore; it was as if Jesus Himself was beckoning for me to come forward.

I took three steps and I saw another woman come forward out of the corner of my eye. *Oh good, I'm not the only one doing this today*, I thought. She came over and gave me a big hug. She wasn't stepping forward; she was a church elder welcoming me into the Body of Christ. Everyone in church began to clap. I started to cry tears of joy for the first time in a long time.

I barely remember driving back home. I did see two birds soar across the sky overhead. They seemed happy and at peace. I knew the feeling for the first time.

ENDNOTE

1. http://biblefacts.org/church/harvest.pdf, 48.

CHAPTER 9

The Potter's Wheel

That peaceful feeling did not last. I suddenly found myself plunged into a foreign world. The first Scripture I heard after I accepted Jesus into my heart was *"Draw near to God and He will draw near to you"* (James 4:8).

What in the world did that mean? Draw near to God? Wasn't He mad at me?

What I didn't realize at the time is that God *had* been drawing me near to Him. Jesus said, *"No one can come to Me unless the Father who sent Me draws him, and I will raise him up at the last day"* (John 6:44 NIV).

When we are traveling on a journey and the road takes twists and turns, it is hard to see the endpoint or visualize the trip. But when you reach the destination and look back, the road map makes sense.

That is how it was for me. As I grew in my Christian faith, I was able to look back over that turbulent year when I first started my business and see God's hand on it all. The removal of my corporate job paved the way for a successful business ministry. Even though we did not have income for part of the year and we were burdened with

Healing in the Hurting Places

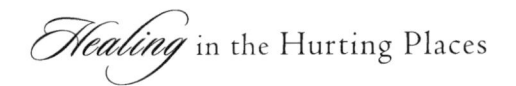

debt, we never lost our house nor wanted for anything. God provided throughout it all.

After years of being independent and stubborn, forging ahead on my own strength, God had to really break my spirit, in order that I become broken enough to receive His. Yes, I had been downcast, depressed, and suicidal, but this was a different breaking process. I was feeling broken because I was having trouble doing things in my own strength.

God's breaking process teaches us that *"...When I am weak, then I am strong"* (2 Cor. 12:10). We are perfected in His strength, not ours. I was trying to do it all on my own; I had no idea that's not how it works. I had a lot of pride and strong will of my own that needed to be broken; I also had yet to learn how to depend on God for all my needs. I had to learn that He was the One who provided them to me.

I think back to that rainy day as I drove to the emergency room in a panic and asked God for His help in locating the hospital. When I looked up and saw it was there all along, I gave credit to the traffic light that had halted my drive, not the God who is truly in the driver's seat.

How many times in our lives do we pray, receive our answer months or years later, and go on our way, never giving thanks to the One who answered our prayer?

With a pulmonary embolism as the third leading cause of instant death in the United States, God kept His hand over us in keeping Bill alive. He was leaving work when he noticed a weak feeling and some trouble drawing air into his lungs. The symptoms could easily have been misinterpreted as shortness of breath or getting up too fast, both of which my husband considered. But instead, he sought immediate medical attention.

In another five minutes, he would have been on a commuter bus traveling through the interstate tunnel. By the time he realized he was in real trouble, it would have been too late. Instead, he was only blocks away from the hospital. It wasn't just any hospital, but one specializing in critical traumas like this. A few years later, the hospital was shut down due to budget cuts. But on that day, every piece of the puzzle was accounted for.

Not only had Bill's life been saved, but my daughter walked away from her serious automobile accident! Yet, despite all of the improbable "coincidences" that God had arranged in my life, I still did not see His hand on the road map. As the prophet Jeremiah proclaimed: *"Hear this, O foolish and senseless people, who have eyes, but do not see; who have ears, but do not hear"* (Jer. 5:21 NASB).

I could not see what was before me. My employee fled with the company's money after I had begun to rebuild my losses. Even that was part of God's plan. I could only see what I was doing in the situation in my own strength and what I had lost. I had no idea what I was about to gain. *"Whoever seeks to keep his life will lose it, and whoever loses his life will preserve it"* (Luke 17:33 NASB).

I am very thankful to God for all of those experiences, even though at the time, I couldn't believe how "unlucky" one person could be. I saw what happened that year as more of a continuation of the abuse and the aftermath that kept me down and unable to get ahead of the pain.

It is only now that I can see how He used even the original rape as a means for His purpose. *"You intended to harm me, but God intended it for good to accomplish what is now being done, the saving of many lives"* (Gen. 50:20 NIV).

Healing in the Hurting Places

Every time I speak to a rape survivor, I silently thank God for the opportunity to speak His Word into her life and bring the chance for hope and healing. If all this had never happened to me, I would not be someone victims could relate to, someone who truly understands what it feels like.

But the road to healing still held many twists and turns.

Although most survivors would probably not admit it, it is hard not to be jealous of others and of what they have when you are always on the outside looking in. Most of the time, I pretended not to notice because there's no sense wanting what you believe will never be yours.

We live in a throwaway society where we have to have the newest, fastest, and coolest toys—be it a cell phone, plasma television, or car. It is all about keeping ahead of the Joneses at an alarming pace. Cell phone manufacturers play into this by offering discounts after you have had your phone for a while and then heavily advertising the latest gadgets and new offerings. This disposable mentality spills over into other areas. So many times I hear, "It's not worth fixing it when I can buy a new and better one."

Jesus warned of this, *"And He said to them, 'Take heed and beware of covetousness, for one's life does not consist in the abundance of the things he possesses'"* (Luke 12:15).

But material things didn't matter to me. What I was jealous of—but also afraid of—were relationships. I really didn't have experience with relationships and I preferred keeping my distance from most people. But there came a point when I started to see the fun that other people were having and realized all that I was missing out on. Deep inside me, an ache started to form.

When I first got saved, the elder who welcomed me to the church sat down with me, gave me a Bible, and suggested that I join a Bible study. I said, "Sure" to be polite, but the last thing I wanted was to go to some stranger's house and do a Bible study. One, I felt inadequate in my knowledge of the Bible. As a child, I had read only parts of it "on the sneak" because we were not supposed to read the Bible.

But mainly, I didn't want to be around other people.

Over the next few months, other Christians began urging me to get involved in "fellowship." As grateful as I was to know that Jesus died for my sins and I would one day be with Him in Heaven, the thought of having to be around other people in a friendly and somewhat intimate environment almost made me want to renounce my salvation.

I know that sounds terrible and I would never have given up that precious gift for anything; but at the time, I really didn't fully appreciate the incredible gift of love and mercy that God had given me. I did get it on some level, but all of the parts of me that hadn't been healed yet didn't know what to do with unconditional love. It was still too overwhelming to take in. The thought of fellowship and being close to other people really scared me.

So many of us come to the Lord late in life; yet even we forget, as time passes, what it is like to be a brand-new Christian. Those who grew up in the Church have very different lives because the Lord is all that they have ever known. Their relationship with God undoubtedly changed over the years and there surely came a point at which they had to make their own personal decisions for Christ; but it is still a very different relationship from those of us who clearly had a "before Christ" and "after Christ" period in our lives.

Second Corinthians 5:17 states: *"Therefore, if anyone is in Christ, he is a new creation; the old has gone, the new has come!"* (NIV). This verse is quoted over and over again to new Christians, almost as a way of convincing them that there is nothing to be concerned about in their past because

Healing in the Hurting Places

it *is* in their past. I have also found in talking to other new Christians, that this is one of the hardest verses to wrap their heads around, because it is not always as easy as flipping a light switch.

They don't understand why old urges, habits, or desires have not dropped off, especially because it does for some at that moment of rebirth. They end up feeling that they did something wrong or that their salvation "didn't take," as one person put it to me.

Worse, if they came from a legalistic church background, they may feel guilt and question their sincerity. I believe that even if you are one of those people who has an immediate transformation, there are still going to be areas in your life that take getting used to.

The prophet Jeremiah was told by the Lord to go to the potter's house so he could observe him:

> *This is the word that came to Jeremiah from the* Lord: *"Go down to the potter's house, and there I will give you My message." So I went down to the potter's house, and I saw him working at the wheel. But the pot he was shaping from the clay was marred in his hands; so the potter formed it into another pot, shaping it as seemed best to him. Then the word of the* Lord *came to me: "O house of Israel, can I not do with you as this potter does?" declares the* Lord. *"Like clay in the hand of the potter, so are you in My hand, O house of Israel"* (Jeremiah 18:1-6 NIV).

When the initial pottery was marred, the potter reshaped it into another vessel. I love this analogy for what the Lord does to us. We are made in His image, but we are born into sin and He remakes us into what He desired for us all along. He does not throw away the misshaped clay of our lives; He recreates us into new beings.

If you have ever watched a potter, the first thing he does is "wedge" the clay. This is the part of the process that requires the most work and is done to remove any imperfections in the clay. Both hands are used during this process as the potter applies force to the clay and literally turns it inside out. He starts out by slamming the clay down on a hard surface and then begins kneading it.

Watching the potter perform these actions had quite an effect on me, especially the first time I saw him powerfully and repeatedly slam the clay down on the table. The sound resonated in me like the bass drums in a funeral march. *Bam! Bam! Bam!* My heart leapt every time the sound was made. There was just something so final and deliberate about it; just as a drum is struck with intended force, the clay was being made to yield any air bubbles or imperfections so the potter could work with it.

My mind went back to one of my favorite passages of Scripture, a story that fascinated me as a child. I would read it over and over again:

Then Saul, still breathing threats and murder against the disciples of the Lord, went to the high priest and asked letters from him to the synagogues of Damascus, so that if he found any who were of the Way, whether men or women, he might bring them bound to Jerusalem. As he journeyed he came near Damascus, and suddenly a light shone around him from heaven. Then he fell to the ground, and heard a voice saying to him, "Saul, Saul, why are you persecuting Me?" And he said, "Who are You, Lord?" Then the Lord said, "I am Jesus, whom you are persecuting. It is hard for you to kick against the goads." So he, trembling and astonished, said, "Lord, what do You want me to do?" Then the Lord said to him, "Arise and go into the city, and you will be told what you must do." And the men who journeyed with him stood speechless, hearing a voice but seeing no one. Then Saul arose from the ground, and when his eyes were opened he saw no one. But they led him by the hand and brought him into Damascus. And he was three days without sight, and neither ate nor drank (Acts 9:1-9).

Healing in the Hurting Places

Our God is a gentle God, kind and merciful. But there are times when He really needs to get our attention. Saul is an example of this. He was so bent on killing Christians. As Scripture words it, he was: *"still breathing threats and murder..."* (Acts 9:1).

Haven't we all felt that way at one time or another? We become so fixated on our goals, our opinions, and our desires, that we decide nothing will stand in our way. We are determined; our hearts are hard, like unworked clay.

At one point in my childhood, I was the fastest runner on the block. Considering that my street was filled with hundreds of kids, this was quite a feat. My winning won everyone's respect, but my style caused them to burst out laughing.

No one else ran like me. And it was part of the reason why I always won.

My whole focus was on one race only, the one in front of me. So instead of running with the confident posture of a marathon runner, I plowed forward, literally. I would run with my body at an angle, my head pointed forward, like a battering ram. I looked like I was about to trip over my feet as I ran.

I raced with everything in me. I ran as if my life depended on it, because running was symbolic to me of the race I had inside. It mirrored my drive to push beyond whatever could potentially defeat me. I needed to win at all costs.

My goal in running was the finish line of finally being accepted by others. It didn't stop at the end of the actual race's finish line. I was driven toward a higher goal.

I'm sure that Saul saw it this way, too. His legacy for killing Christians was well-known. He, too, was "bent" on getting across his imaginary finish line. And so God had to strike him off his horse. *Bam!* To fully get his attention, he was struck blind for three days, giving him plenty of time to think about things in the darkness.

I understand this all too well. God has needed to strike me a few times to fully get my attention. He does this because He loves us that much. Sometimes He needs to take us from where we've been and strike us hard against the table so He can begin to soften us up and get us ready for the process that lies ahead.

The wedging process forces the clay to be made uniform so it can be worked on the wheel. When we become Christians, we too, are made uniform in that, regardless of our pasts and sins, we are all now blood brothers and sisters in Christ. We have been bought with a price and all of us now have that inalienable right to eternal life.

To test the uniformity of the clay, the potter cuts the clay with a sharp-edged knife. This reveals what is inside the clay. So too, the Word of God has been compared to a two-edged sword, made to reveal what is inside us:

For the word of God is living and powerful, and sharper than any two-edged sword, piercing even to the division of soul and spirit, and of joints and marrow, and is a discerner of the thoughts and intents of the heart. And there is no creature hidden from His sight, but all things are naked and open to the eyes of Him to whom we must give account (Hebrews 4:12-13).

Next the potter takes the clay and "centers" it on the wheel. Potters are taught that unless the clay is centered, the piece will not turn out right. Establishing the proper foundation is essential to the process. Jesus taught us this principle of making sure our foundation is solid and centered on His Word:

Healing in the Hurting Places

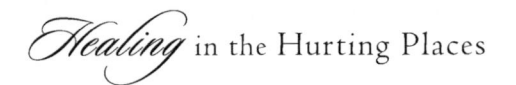

Therefore whoever hears these sayings of Mine, and does them, I will liken him to a wise man who built his house on the rock: and the rain descended, the floods came, and the winds blew and beat on that house; and it did not fall, for it was founded on the rock. But everyone who hears these sayings of Mine, and does not do them, will be like a foolish man who built his house on the sand: and the rain descended, the floods came, and the winds blew and beat on that house; and it fell. And great was its fall (Matthew 7:24-27).

The clay is most resistant at this stage on the wheel. The potter still fights with the clay as he forces it to become centered, but God is a gentleman and will not enter in without being asked. *"Behold, I stand at the door and knock. If anyone hears My voice and opens the door, I will come in to him and dine with him, and he with Me"* (Rev. 3:20). Once He has been invited into our hearts, He will apply the needed pressure to conform us into the desired goal. We, too, will fight at this stage.

Sadly, I probably put up my strongest battles against God. But I also believe it was because He was allowing me the freedom to find a voice where I'd never had one before. He allowed me to exercise that voice along with my free will, so that it could be released. Then I would be ready to yield to Him. Unless we allow God to become the center of our lives, we will continue to fight the plans He has for us and the good that He has in store for us.

This became one of the ultimate challenges for me during the healing process; could I give the reins that I held onto so tightly and turn them over to God? Could I learn to look to Him for every provision of my life, to allow Him to be the center without hesitation? Could I stop running the race for acceptance and learn to run the race for the prize of His glory?

The Potter's Wheel

When Saul, who became Paul, had his eyes opened, he learned to focus on the true finish line:

I press on to reach the end of the race and receive the heavenly prize for which God, through Christ Jesus, is calling us (Philippians 3:14 NLT).

Once we realize that only God can fill that hole in our lives, that all of the other stuff—success, alcohol, sex, drugs, pornography, money—will leave us wanting and empty. God can then begin to shape us. So too, the potter, once the clay has been centered, will reach into that hole and begin to mold the clay.

As the clay begins to take shape, less pressure needs to be applied by the potter as he begins to gently guide the piece. It becomes abundantly clear why the Lord sent Jeremiah to observe the potter. When we start to follow God's will freely and seek His direction for our lives, the journey becomes easier and more visible. As events unfold, we start understanding a small piece of the plan that God has for our lives.

If the potter takes his hand off the clay at this point, it will remain unfinished—and unusable. It may still contain imperfections that need to be cut away by the potter's skillful hands. There may be unwanted pieces inside that the potter needs to reach in deep to remove. The Potter will do all these things for us, if we allow Him.

When the clay comes off the wheel, it is still fragile until it is put in the kiln and fired. The firing process exposes the piece to extreme heat for extended periods of time, which changes the makeup of the clay and allows it to become something that can be used.

Anyone who has ever been through a fiery trial can attest to the pressure and discomfort felt in the process. It has always felt like too long of a time period for me, yet I marvel at the results He has achieved through it when the trial is over. We are not ready to be used unless we have been fired and tested in our lives.

Healing in the Hurting Places

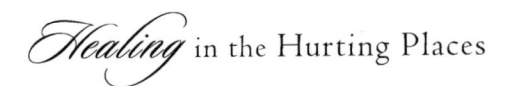

I feel that God always does His best work through the darkest trials, as He prepares us to be used for His purposes. Just as diamonds are formed from pressure, and steel forged through heat, we too become God's pièce de résistance when we emerge from the fire, just like the pottery.

CHAPTER 10

Bathed in Son Light

Relationships continued to be one of the hardest parts of the initial process. Once I became more honest and open about my feelings, I had to learn when to speak out and when to use restraint. Before this, I kept my feelings and thoughts locked behind a well-gated fortress. My conversations were guarded and professional, for the most part. After leaving high school and settling down, I had few friends. I knew the parents of the children my kids played with, but there was never any intimate conversation. Most of my friends from high school moved away. I didn't associate with the people I worked with.

My insecurities in this area, coupled with my history of "doing good" on a large scale, resulted in some misfirings. My overzealousness to fulfill the Great Commission found me writing three-page letters at Christmastime to my old friends from school telling them how I had found Jesus. While this is great news to share, the letters were written in my "over the top" style. I had suddenly turned into one of those in-your-face born-again Christians who can turn some people off.

Healing in the Hurting Places

When I first discovered my new church on their Website, it was listed as "non-denominational." That was nonconfrontational to me and so I was willing to go. Had I realized it was a "born-again church" I would not have gone.

This was due to several encounters in my youth with overzealous born-again Christians. The most traumatic was a young Vacation Bible School (VBS) teacher who locked each of us in a room and would not let us out until we accepted Jesus. While locked in, he told us how we had to give up all of our false idols—singers, Hollywood stars we liked, candy, sports, television, music, etc., or else we would go straight to hell.

It's hard for an 11-year-old to hear that having a David Cassidy poster on her wall is going to condemn her to life in hell. I wasn't worshiping him; I just thought he looked kind of cute and I enjoyed his songs. I'm sure the teacher's intent was good and I was probably too young to comprehend all that he was saying, but I would have agreed to almost anything to be let out of that room.

For a sexual abuse survivor to be locked in a room with a young man breathing in her face and trying to force her to agree to do something against her will was unbearable.

While my three-page Christmas letter was not *that* overbearing, I'm sure that I came across to others with the passion of my past rather than the passion of Christ. I still had much to learn about the Christian walk. I remember someone around this time pointing out to me that there was a reason why it was called a "walk" and not a "run." For me, a recovering run-aholic, the metaphor was simply perfect.

It has been said to preach the Gospel always, and when necessary, use words.

Bathed in Son Light

I think it takes some time in the Lord to develop a sense of His purpose for your life and how you can be used by Him. That isn't to say that people can't be led to the Lord by brand-new Christians, but the reality is, none of us saves anyone. That is God's role, alone. All we are called to do is be salt and light. We plant the seeds and He waters them. Sometimes, it takes some time to figure how we go about planting those seeds.

My biggest detriment was striving. While I had the peace of Christ in me, I was far from being at peace. I was still operating under the impression that I had to do something. Even being Christian gave me new things to "do"—ministries to join, Bible studies to take, classes to sign up for.

The Bible studies proved to be tough. These folks wanted to share their hearts and mine was still under lock and key. They also free-framed prayers, like that night on the beach. I was terrified to pray aloud. For almost a year, my vocalized prayers sounded stiff and formal, while my personal prayers were becoming easier every day. Then a sister in the Lord took me aside and told me to just talk to Him as if I were the only one in the room. In other words, my group prayers could sound just like those silent ones!

Later, I learned about praying God's Word back to Him. If someone was visiting from a foreign country, we would probably make an attempt to talk to them in their native language, even if we could only muster a few words. We would want them to feel comfortable and able to relate to us. While God is not looking for us to make Him feel comfortable, I think using the words He gave us shows honor and reverence. The Bible is full of ways to praise Him.

Too often our prayers are requests for things we want, not seeking the will of God or praising Him for all of our blessings. I think about how, after 20 years in the corporate world, in seven different fields and

Healing in the Hurting Places

surviving four layoffs, I now have my own business. Every morning, I wake up and get to do what I feel passionate about, while using the talents God gave me to minister to others. How blessed I am! If I ever need something to thank God for when I am praying, I can always fall back on this, especially when we consider that 75 percent of the workforce in America trudges daily to jobs they despise.

God was kind and gentle to me during this period as I look back now. He softly molded and guided me like that piece of clay, as I allowed my heart to gradually soften. He let me acclimate to my new church, praying aloud, and starting to open up to people. But He also pressed for my obedience. That was especially tough for me.

One of the first requests God made of me was to trust. Trust is one of the hardest challenges for sexual abuse survivors. They have been too hurt, too violated, too scarred to ever let themselves be that vulnerable again. The way I looked at it, the few times that I toyed with trusting showed me that it was just not worth it.

But God would not let up. And when I did, the results were far more damaging than I could have ever envisioned. As a brand-new Christian, I questioned every move. *Had I really heard from God? Did I not understand the instructions? Had I executed incorrectly?*

God's plan had already been put into play and it was too late to stop. The domino effect from that step of obedience by trusting as He had directed caused layers of problems. It was years before I could step back and see the results of God's plan and how that step was exactly the one that needed to be taken at that moment in time. So much of what I am thankful for now began with that one act of obedience.

But it was always like that...

After these things the word of the LORD *came to Abram in a vision, saying, "Do not be afraid, Abram. I am your shield, your exceedingly great* *reward." But Abram said, "Lord G*OD*, what will You give me, seeing I go childless, and the heir of my house is Eliezer of Damascus?" Then Abram said, "Look, You have given me no offspring; indeed one born in my house is my heir!" And behold, the word of the L*ORD *came to him, saying, "This one shall not be your heir, but one who will come from your own body shall be your heir." Then He brought him outside and said, "Look now toward heaven, and count the stars if you are able to number them." And He said to him, "So shall your descendants be." And he believed in the L*ORD*, and He accounted it to him for righteousness* (Genesis 15:1-6).

Abram trusted and believed in God. But his wife, Sarai, decided to take matters into her own hands. She suggested to Abram that he lie with her maidservant, Hagar, and conceive a child that way, which he did (see Gen. 16).

But jumping ahead of God and acting on your own strength in disobedience to God brings consequences. Sin might feel good initially, but it ultimately destroys and poisons. Once Hagar conceived, Sarai began to despise her and eventually drove her away (see Gen. 21).

But God still had plans for Abram and Sarai and made a covenant with them. There were a number of commandments that He asked them to obey. And then He blessed them with a son, Isaac. As we follow their story, we see the ups and down of a couple trying to obey the Lord, while struggling in their own sins and human condition. For example, Sarai laughed when she first heard that she was going to conceive. She then tried to deny it, yet God still blessed her. But first He confronted her dishonesty (see Gen. 18:12-15).

God wants to see us excel in His Kingdom, but He cannot look upon and condone the face of sin. There will be new trials to strengthen and fortify us that will change the underlying characteristics that still need refining. Abraham underwent a difficult trial in the shaping of his character.

Healing in the Hurting Places

At the age of 99, God gave a son, Isaac, to Abraham. And then He made this request of him:

> *Now it came to pass after these things that God tested Abraham, and said to him, "Abraham!" And he said, "Here I am." Then He said, "Take now your son, your only son Isaac, whom you love, and go to the land of Moriah, and offer him there as a burnt offering on one of the mountains of which I shall tell you." So Abraham rose early in the morning and saddled his donkey, and took two of his young men with him, and Isaac his son; and he split the wood for the burnt offering, and arose and went to the place of which God had told him...And Abraham built an altar there and placed the wood in order; and he bound Isaac his son and laid him on the altar, upon the wood. And Abraham stretched out his hand and took the knife to slay his son. But the Angel of the LORD called to him from heaven and said, "Abraham, Abraham!" So he said, "Here I am." And He said, "Do not lay your hand on the lad, or do anything to him; for now I know that you fear God, since you have not withheld your son, your only son, from Me."...Then the Angel of the LORD called to Abraham a second time out of heaven, and said: "By Myself I have sworn, says the LORD, because you have done this thing, and have not withheld your son, your only son—blessing I will bless you, and multiplying I will multiply your descendants as the stars of the heaven and as the sand which is on the seashore; and your descendants shall possess the gate of their enemies. In your seed all the nations of the earth shall be blessed, because you have obeyed My voice"* (Genesis 22:1-3;9-12;15-18).

As my first year in the Lord drew to a close, I saw God's blessings, as well as the requests He made upon my life. I watched how He shaped me during that first year. Others around me began to notice the softening up and change in me. I was not as frantic and anxious anymore.

I was crying—real tears—and I couldn't shut them off. I was allowing people in church to get close enough to hug me, and I was learning that it could be healing. It seemed that with every tear I shed and every hug I got, another stone in the fortress crumbled.

It is reported that a study done by William Frey showed that tears released during an emotional situation contained levels of cortisol—the stress hormone—while tears that flowed in other situations like the cutting of an onion, did not.[1] Our emotional tears are designed by God to flush away the toxins produced during stressful scenarios. I didn't learn about this study until after many tears had fallen. I am thankful for the One who designed a way for me to release the emotions and pain that had held me bound for so long.

But tears weren't the only watery component I was facing. My pastor had several discussions with me regarding baptism. Having been baptized already as a 15-day-old infant, I saw no need to repeat the process. He explained to me that it is different when you make a choice as an adult, but I dismissed it as ritualistic.

At the beach, I heard a pastor talk about baptism being an outward sign of the changes God had made inwardly, a way to proclaim and testify to all that He had done in the believer's life. My heart cracked open that day and I knew that I wanted to do this with all that was in me. The restraint that had bound my heart no longer held me captive; I was ready to truly proclaim Jesus as my Lord and Savior.

Ocean baptisms were being conducted that evening. I ran down the beach, this time with my head held high, as I took my place as first on line. (I still had some work to do in the striving area.) I never liked putting my head underwater since a kid in summer camp pushed me under at a public pool and I nearly drowned. I remember opening my eyes and seeing the bottom of the pool. I never again swam with my eyes open. I had never really mastered my fear of the water and was a poor swimmer at best. I explained my fear of the water to the pastors waiting to pray with me and baptize me. While full immersion was the protocol, they understood my fear and told me that they could dip the back of my head in the water to alleviate any concerns I had.

"Oh no," I told them. "I want to go completely under. I want to do this for my Lord and Savior for all that He has done for me."

They smiled, prayed with me, and led me out into the ocean. I held my nose as they leaned me back in the water. When my head was fully under, I opened my eyes. It was a beautiful summer day and the rays of the sun were shining through the semi-clear Atlantic Ocean. As I watched the waves pass over my face, I felt as if the warmth of Christ was spreading across me. My body relaxed as peace and tranquility flowed through my body, as the Son shone on my face.

ENDNOTE

1. Paula Becker, "The Healing Power of Tears," CyQuest, http://wwwcyquest.com/motherhome/healing_power_of_tears.html, accessed July 5, 2010.

Chapter 11

Out of the Comfort Zone

Now that the Lord had started to soften my heart and I was ready to accept Him as my all in all, I was in a place where He could really work with me. It was like He was now reaching into the center of that wedge of clay and shaping me into what He had planned for my life. But, in the early stages, I was still fighting Him.

I often think back now to that day of my baptism. How the waters washed over me and I was not afraid because I felt His love. The author of Lamentations understood this:

The waters flowed over my head; I said, "I am cut off!" I called on Your name, O LORD, from the lowest pit. You have heard my voice: "Do not hide Your ear from my sighing, from my cry for help." You drew near on the day I called on You, and said, "Do not fear!" (Lamentations 3:54-57)

I was able to relate to the "lowest pit" experience; I understood crying out to the Lord. First, He taught me, and allowed me, to cry again; then in His gracious mercy, He showed me how to cry out to Him.

Healing in the Hurting Places

I look back over the five years since I accepted Jesus in my heart and I see these peaks and valleys. Some may compare it to labor pains. The pain comes, the contraction becomes stronger, then it eases off and you have a little break to catch your breath and relax before the next one. At the end comes the reward that makes all that pain worthwhile.

My first year was an initiation, not unlike the initial stages of any relationship. Slowly, gingerly, you get to know one another. You learn where the boundaries are and you slowly let down your guard and let the other person see your heart.

Of course, in the case of God, He knew my heart all the time, since He formed it in the first place and knew me before the foundations of the earth. I find it comforting to have a Father who knows all about me:

> *For You formed my inward parts; You covered me in my mother's womb. I will praise You, for I am fearfully and wonderfully made; marvelous are Your works, and that my soul knows very well. My frame was not hidden from You, when I was made in secret, and skillfully wrought in the lowest parts of the earth. Your eyes saw my substance, being yet unformed. And in Your book they all were written, the days fashioned for me, when as yet there were none of them. How precious also are Your thoughts to me, O God! How great is the sum of them! If I should count them, they would be more in number than the sand; when I awake, I am still with You* (Psalm 139:13-18).

Shortly after the "breather" in the Atlantic where God's presence was felt that day, He brought me into my first big trial. It was finally time to deal with the pain of the past. I had no intentions of opening that up again. As far as I was concerned, I had done all the therapy, read all the books, and experienced all the flashbacks that I wanted in regard to those experiences. I was ready to celebrate my new life in Christ. There was a whole new world waiting for me.

But the potter knows that he will never fire the piece that is still filled inside with gunk that doesn't belong there. It may not be visible from the outside, but it is there nonetheless and the pottery will never be as beautiful as it could be unless the gunk is removed.

So God got busy scrubbing the gunk from my life.

I had processed my past on an intellectual level. I made the decisions that needed to be made to forge ahead. Every move was as calculated as possible. My heart was detached. But it was my heart that was hurting and that is what needed to be healed.

One day, when I was about nine or ten, my friends and I were playing in the "older kids" playground. Instead of the smaller slides and little, gentle rides found in the other playground for the younger set, the equipment here was scaled for the size of adolescents. It was adjacent to the basketball and softball fields where the older kids played. It was a big treat to be there.

This was also back in the days before playgrounds were made safer to prevent lawsuits. Our swings were heavy, clunky metal ones. If you walked in front of someone swinging, you got a nice bruise on your head—if you didn't get knocked out altogether. Either way, you learned never to do that again.

The slides were straight and made of metal that got really hot in the sun, not twisty and plastic like the ones of today. They were about ten feet high and you would go down pretty fast because of the straight, smooth surface and pitch of the slide. Because of this, my friends and I would hold races, seeing who could run up the steps and slide down the fastest.

Healing in the Hurting Places

One day, workers were doing repairs and had placed a wooden board across part of the metal slide area. The slide should have been cordoned off and perhaps it was when the workers left it, but it was open when I arrived. I grabbed that slide and raced my friend. Since it was summer, I was wearing light shorts and I wound up with a nice wooden splinter about an inch long in my buttocks. The pitch of the slide forced it in at an angle, so it went deep into the epidermis. It smarted, but of course, I was tough about it and said nothing. I was also actually ashamed and didn't want anyone to see it. So I ignored it, thinking it would go away for some reason.

It didn't. It actually became infected. And it worked its way even deeper into my skin. Eventually, I told my sister, who was a nurse, about it. She had to really dig in to remove the splinter at that point because so many layers of skin had formed over it. If I had let her or someone else take it out immediately, I would not have suffered with it the way that I did. It probably could have been pulled out through the original break in the skin. But now, because it had to be cut out, I was left with a scar that I still have, and always will.

This is similar to the condition of my heart. I ignored the pain in it and, over time, layers formed over the pain until it wasn't noticeable to me anymore. But that didn't mean it wasn't there. I could try to forget about it, but the discomfort was always with me. In time, I just learned to live with it. But it needed to come out in order to heal.

The removal of that splinter was rather painful, because all of those layers had to be cut away. It developed an infection that spread to the surrounding area because it had been left unchecked. Likewise, the pain of my past had also spread like a sickness. It left a scar because the wound had grown so deep.

None of this was healthy. So God began to work with me to open up and clean out the wound in my heart.

Out of the Comfort Zone

A dear sister in the Lord once shared the analogy of a beach ball with me. The harder you try to hold a beach ball under the water, the more it will want to pop up. But no matter how hard or how little you try, the ball will come to the surface. And if you hold it down too far or too hard, it will pop up out of the water with great force, splashing everyone.

As silly as it may sound, this is a great description of my life at that time. It was like one giant beach ball waiting to burst out of the water; even though I did my best to hold it down, it popped up with considerable force and soaked everyone around it.

I had been very focused on keeping that ball under the water. Once my efforts failed, it was game over. Anxiety and growing unrest would pop up at a moment's notice. I could be calmly working one minute and be completely set off the next by an email regarding a complaint or problem. It didn't have to be a big problem. I guess the best way to describe my feelings at the time is *hypervigilant*.

As things came to the surface, my nerves became frayed and my patience waned. As the pain from the past unraveled from inside my heart, it created more anxiety and unrest within me. I had built my foundation on the sinking sand of my own control. Now God was removing my hands from the control panel, finger by finger.

At night, it was hard to turn off the anxiety. I would toss and turn and lie awake for hours thinking about all the stuff being brought to the surface. Added to that were thoughts about behaviors that made me uncomfortable, such as my loss of control or my demonstrations of impatience in situations I would have handled "better" in the past. My guilt over how I had acted began to increase exponentially.

The sleepless nights took their toll in the daytime. I was less able to concentrate and my judgment was off because I was not well-rested.

Healing in the Hurting Places

I later learned that the immune system functions while we sleep. When we have broken sleep, we are more susceptible to sickness, because the immune system is not functioning at its peak. I didn't find myself getting sick more often, but when I did, I felt like I didn't have the reserves to properly fight it off.

The crying was still an issue. All of a sudden, I was dealing with all of these tears—happy tears, sad tears, tears from stress. I felt like I did more crying in my first few years of becoming a Christian than in all my life before that. And because this was new terrain for me, I was not comfortable with it. Of course, I know now that I was not supposed to be at ease; God was nudging me out of my comfort zone.

It was getting harder and harder for me to find God in this picture. It seemed like since I had become a Christian, my whole world had been rocked. I look back now and say "Praise God!" At the time, however, it was all very confusing and even frightening in some ways, because we are all very much creatures of habit.

I kept trying to read the Bible, but the deeper I dug, the more confusing it became. I was gifted with a study Bible around that time—an appropriate gift that still serves me well. This helped me to start unpacking some of what I was reading. I was still taking Bible studies, but so much of what was said went over my head. After a while, I felt like I was holding everyone back by asking so many questions. But they were all gracious and understanding about it.

This became another hard area for me: understanding people. The Christians in my life were so different from the people I had always known. Most of my world had either been filled with people in pain, like I was, or people I never got to know beneath the surface. They tended to be more coarse, impatient, cynical, and harsher.

The Christians I met were more peaceful, upbeat, patient, and understanding. It was a sharp contrast that unnerved me. They were also much more open and affectionate. I was not used to being hugged, but in time, I began to welcome these kind gestures.

It's not that Christians are any different than the rest of us; we all have our bad days and times when we are not acting as Jesus would. But the difference I've learned is pressing into Him—giving Him what we cannot do in our own strength. The true joy of the Lord comes from realizing as Jesus told us: *"My yoke is easy and My burden is light"* (Matt. 11:30 NIV).

We try to make things harder than they need to be, but God never asked that of us. In fact, He asked the opposite, saying, *"I tell you the truth, unless you change and become like little children, you will never enter the kingdom of heaven"* (Matt. 18:3 NIV).

Just when my discouragement and unrest would reach an all-time high, God would surprise me. One day, I had a very difficult phone conversation and was rather distraught. I was at a new church and walked past a man at the information booth. He seemed like a natural there and immediately picked up on my emotions. He began talking to me as if we had known each other for years. It was very comfortable, relaxing, and calming to my anxious heart. I could see why they had put a man like that at a booth in the entrance hall.

After a wonderful 20-minute carefree conversation, the pastor came along and tapped my shoulder. I excused myself for a moment and when I turned back, my new friend was gone. I thought it odd that he left his assignment at the booth with service starting in five minutes.

I later found out that he was not the information booth servant and had never been in that role. He was actually part of the praise and worship team. At the precise moment that I pulled into the parking lot, there was a problem with the sound equipment and he had come out to the booth to look for a screwdriver. That was when I walked in. Seeing my distress, he never let on that he was in a hurry and needed to fix the equipment before service. He simply became "Jesus with skin on" and let God worry about the time and the sound equipment.

I have learned from that experience and many others that God will always restore the time that we spend in service to Him. One of my life verses is *"So I will restore to you the years that the swarming locust has eaten..."* (Joel 2:25) and I have watched Him do that time and time again in my own and others' lives.

Moments like this kept me anchored while life's turbulent seas tossed me around. But all of this weepiness, insomnia, and anxiety had yet to prepare me for what was to come.

Chapter 12

Wrath and Forgiveness

Little by little, I confided in a few people about the abuse I had suffered. My new family of Christian brothers and sisters were helping me to feel at ease around people. I was learning to be less paranoid, meticulous, and controlling, and was becoming more at ease around others.

I noticed an interesting trend: When I told women what happened to me, they would usually give sympathetic responses. But when men heard my story, almost universally, the initial reaction would be one of anger. I just assumed that men were more comfortable with anger, just like women were more comfortable with tears. But as I conversed more with the women, I found out that they were angry, too.

No one seemed to understand how I could avoid being angry for what had happened to me. I assured them that I never had any anger about the situation. *What would that prove?*

One night during a healing session, the counselors encouraged me to express my hidden feelings. One by one, they ticked off potential

Healing in the Hurting Places

candidates: disappointment, hurt, loneliness, sorrow... Each time I expressed a specific emotion that I had experienced and stored up inside, I was supposed to think about it and visualize handing it over to Jesus, who would take it from my life.

When the counselors got to anger, I hesitated for the first time and tried to say that I didn't have any anger. But I got stuck there. I had never believed that I had anger, so there was no need to hand it over. I thought, *You can't hand over something you don't have to give.*

But I was going deep with God on this exercise and letting Him guide my heart. And I found that I couldn't move on. Something was stopping me. It was a very eerie moment in which time seemed to stand still.

It was as though I were fighting with myself. Part of me deep, deep down knew the truth, and God knew it, too. But the rest of me was in such denial that I couldn't see that deep part. Suddenly, an endless stream of words tumbled out of me. I talked about the anger I didn't know I had. For almost half an hour, I vocalized nonstop with deep emotion all the things I was angry about.

In many ways, it was like a huge burden was lifted from my shoulders that night. But in other ways, it was just the beginning of a long saga, because I now knew about all of the pent-up rage inside of me. I had never dealt with or expressed it before and I had no idea how to handle it.

Growing up, I never learned how to deal with anger. We weren't allowed to express such an emotion in our household. There was only one time I ever recall either of my parents getting angry. My father went into the other room, closed the door, and vented privately. Then he came back into the room as though nothing had happened. It made me extremely uncomfortable and sent a debilitating unspoken message: Anger is bad; anger is wrong; anger should never be expressed in front of anyone.

Wrath and Forgiveness

When my kids, who are fairly close in age, began to squabble and engage in normal sibling rivalry, I panicked. I felt as though I'd failed as a mother. I didn't understand why my kids "hated" each other. So entrenched was the negative attitude toward anger that I thought there was something wrong in having this emotion.

It took a lot of counseling, reading books, and consulting with brothers, sisters, and leaders in the church before I could begin to understand anger. I freely admit that I still have a lot to learn and a long way to go with this emotion.

Quite frankly, I am afraid of it. When someone is angry with me, nothing is right in my world. My immediate reaction is to retreat and remove myself from the situation, much the way my father did that day. But even if I do, I want to come right back and resolve something with the person who is angry with me. I want things right in my world again and right between us. And even if we do discuss it and come to terms, I will be sensitive and concerned for a brief time about the aftermath. My heart will ache for having had the argument to begin with.

Some people are competitive, some are argumentative, and some take disagreements in stride. I'm not sure I will ever be in the last group. I'm just not comfortable with disagreements, period. And I've talked to a lot of abuse survivors who feel the same way. I think because so many of us did not have the happy endings in our childhood that our storybooks promised us, we want happy endings as adults.

I don't have a problem owning and admitting anything I may have done wrong to provoke the anger or continue the argument. I am willing to admit where I have shortcomings and where I have failed the other person. This did not come naturally, but over time, God showed and taught me the importance of this. The Bible exhorts us along these lines: *"Confess your sins to one another and pray for one another, so that you may be healed..."* (James 5:16 HCSB).

Healing in the Hurting Places

My initial reaction was always to apologize, and even over-apologize, just to maintain peace. This is not sincere and was something God had to break me of. Now, while it sometimes frustrates me to fail so often, I see how God uses this issue in my life to minister to others. If we look perfect, then others won't see themselves in us or feel we are approachable. Also, if we are more concerned with how we look than with making things right, we can rest assured that pride is at work.

Part of owning the issues in my own backyard meant seeing anger in all of its forms. We can easily recognize rage, but there are more subtle forms of anger, such as pouting, controlling, manipulating, and giving someone the silent treatment. When I learned this through counseling, I was able to see that I had been angry for a lot longer than I realized.

Forgiving the other person has proven to be a bit more daunting. Our flesh wants remorse, restitution, and even retaliation. But God's Word says:

Never take your own revenge, beloved, but leave room for the wrath of God, for it is written, "VENGEANCE IS MINE, I WILL REPAY," says the Lord (Romans 12:19 NASB).

Forgiving others was hard, but forgiving myself was probably the greatest challenge. Because I had always been so hard on myself, this did not come easy. I couldn't see how I deserved forgiveness. I expressed this once to a pastor who smiled, clapped me on the back, and assured me that I would never be *worthy* of forgiveness. And that, in essence, is the point of the cross.

As I mature in my understanding of anger, I find I am no longer willing to be a doormat. I respect the person who owns their anger and whatever wrong they may have done, and is willing to put forth an apology. I lose respect for those who can't let go of their pride and do this. But in either case, I will forgive them.

Wrath and Forgiveness

I am not saying this is easy. I am not saying that I always do this willingly. It has been a transformation in progress. I have gone from a place of being willing to do anything to resolve an argument, to sticking up for myself, and standing my ground so I am not walked on. From there, I had to balance the doormat versus pride and learn how to walk in His light between the two.

I've been told that forgiveness is about freedom—and the person who is set free is usually yourself. When we refuse to forgive others, we make ourselves a prisoner of our own stubborn pride. Our hearts become hard. We seldom realize how damaging it is not to forgive others; it is like a poison that spreads and does further damage to ourselves and others. It may be hard to forgive someone who has not recognized their error or how they may have harmed you, but we have been asked to forgive, nonetheless. When you release the other person, it is you who walks out of bondage. Praying for someone with whom you were (or still are) angry is one of the hardest things to do. Yet, when we are centered on ourselves and then shift to ministering to others, our problems seem to diminish and we are blessed. This is also true with praying for others against whom you may have resentment.

I remember when one of my sisters in the Lord suggested praying for the person I was having trouble forgiving. At first, I thought the idea was preposterous and dismissed it. But the Holy Spirit kept prodding me. The situation wasn't getting any better, so I almost entered into it out of desperation.

Someone once said, "God will take you any way He can get you," and that held true here. My motives might not have been pure at the beginning, but as I steadfastly prayed for this person, my attitude began to change. Suddenly, I saw all of the good in this person—all of which I had been blinded to while in my unforgiving state. God helped me to remember all of the good things the person had done for me and I started to feel guilty and ashamed.

The struggle with forgiveness is formidable, but the ultimate test comes when we have to face the cross and acknowledge that Jesus died for sins He never committed. It is hard to grasp that He loved us enough to use His own body to purchase forgiveness for *our* sins. If He could forgive us, who are we not to forgive others? This sobering thought has allowed me to let go of any resentment or lingering unforgiveness.

Another part of the healing journey is to confess your sins to those you have harmed and try to make amends whenever possible to restore the relationship. Even though I was the victim of sexual abuse, I made others my victims when I lashed out at them or turned my pain on them. Although I didn't wake up in the morning saying, "I'm going to hurt this person emotionally and make them feel bad because I am hurting," my actions produced that very result.

Jesus calls us to be accountable for all of our actions. Whether the act was willful or not makes no difference. Unfortunately, accountability is taking a backseat these days. We hear the *sin* word less and less. For example, adultery is a sin which, in Old Testament days, was punishable by stoning the offender to death. Today, it is referred to as "a little indiscretion," "a one-night stand," or something that "just happened." Sometimes, we even try to make it sound exotic, as in, "We have an open marriage."

We've replaced the word *accountable* with *justifiable*. Defense lawyers try to get their clients off because they were raised in broken homes, grew up in poor circumstances, were bullied, etc. While all of these factors can certainly affect behavior, in the end, we alone are ultimately responsible for what we do.

Wrath and Forgiveness

Shrugging off our responsibility is as old as the story of Cain and Abel. When Cain killed his brother Abel in a fit of jealousy, his distress came not from what he did, but from the punishment he received from God. When God first questioned Cain as to where his brother was, Cain lied and said sarcastically, *"I do not know. Am I my brother's keeper?"* (Gen. 4:9).

We are all our brothers' keepers. Paul cautions us not to *"...do anything by which your brother stumbles or is offended or is made weak"* (Rom. 14:21). He goes on to exhort us: *"Let each of us please his neighbor for his good, leading to edification"* (Rom. 15:2).

Instead, too many of us try to justify our actions, like Cain or the accused person on trial. We point to past abuse as an excuse for our behavior. This is something I did for years without realizing it. I knew what had happened to me and I saw the resulting behavior; I expected others to be understanding of this. *If this had happened to them, they would act the same way*, I told myself.

If the other person was a Christian, I unfairly held them to an even higher standard. The problem isn't that we shouldn't aspire to higher standards; it's when we expect or impose our ideals on others and demand, even subconsciously, that they live up to them. I remember even thinking at one point, if they are having so much trouble dealing with this, all they have to do is ask God for the strength they lack.

I couldn't take the next step in the healing process until I realized that it was I who needed to change. The only person we can change is ourselves. Often, when people marry, they try to change the personality of the person with whom they fell in love. Married or not, we humans tend to push this "retraining behavior" on those around us.

Being creatures of habit, we become conditioned to the elements in our environment. When we force someone to change by subtly changing

Healing in the Hurting Places

the elements of that environment or act or say things in a certain way to affect the desired result, we are manipulating the other person.

I came from a manipulative home environment. I could see the erroneous behavior there so clearly and never wanted to be like that, but I couldn't see it in myself when I did it to others. I would say something a certain way, convinced in my own mind that I was just conversing. But the end result was based on what I expected the other person to say or do. I didn't recognize that I was actually altering my words and tone of voice to achieve my desired result.

One of the things that helped me was to leave a tape recorder running during the course of the day. I was shocked to hear how I spoke to others and immediately understood why actions that were invisible to me were so apparent to others. They were clearly recorded as evidence of my manipulation!

Another way a victim can use justification is as an excuse for what the rapist did to him or her. Many pedophiles and abusers were abused themselves as children. In my case, I knew the perpetrator was abused as a child and so I justified his behavior as being unavoidable; he was simply unable to stop himself and was only doing what he had been taught to do.

The truth is that there is never a reason to perpetuate abuse. I didn't sexually abuse others and many other victims don't, either. Yes, a high number of abusers do continue the cycle, but that is not an acceptable excuse. Many alcoholics come from families of alcoholics, but they must seek the means to stop drinking on their own. If everyone continued the cycle, ultimately, we would become an entire planet of abusers!

Chapter 13

Transparency

It was the second evening of a three-day retreat. That afternoon, the facilitator had asked for volunteers to give their testimonies. I was a fairly new Christian, but God had made a lot of changes in my life since I gave my heart to Him two years earlier. I added my name to the list.

Back in my room, I made notes on the hotel pad about what I wanted to say. Then I lay down on the floor in surrender and asked Jesus to use me in any way that He saw fit, to give me the words that He wanted me to say. A strange sensation came over me. Somewhere in my gut, I didn't think I was going to say the words I had just scribbled on the pad. But I didn't have a clue what I was going to say instead.

As we lined up in the back to await our turn, one of my friends leaned over and said, "Are you ready? Do you know what you are going to say?"

"I thought I did, but now I'm not so sure," I replied.

Healing in the Hurting Places

It was my turn. I went up there with the notes I had made earlier. I had committed a speech to memory and the notes would help jog it if I hesitated. Still...that strange feeling from the hotel room lingered in my gut.

I looked out in the audience and smiled. I was the author of two books and had given hundreds of talks. I was used to giving speeches and I had many friends in the audience. But as I adjusted the podium microphone, I felt very intimidated.

"Good evening everyone," I started, as I smiled at them.

"Good evening," they replied in unison.

As I unfolded my speech, my hands felt clammy. I glanced at the words—the opening joke, the things that Christ had shown me over the past two years, some analogies, what impact this retreat had made on me so far—and then I folded the paper up again. I could feel their eyes upon me, waiting for me to start. I cleared my throat.

"I had written out some notes to share with you tonight, but as I stand here, I feel like God is telling me to say something else. I honestly don't know what I am about to say, but I feel like there is someone here tonight whom this message is for.

"When I was a child, I was sexually abused..." I went on to share the pain of my past and the pain of my present as I dealt with what had happened. I talked about Luke and seeing the speck in your brother's eye while missing the plank in your own. I spoke about how I was so caught in all of the emotions of processing what had happened to me, I didn't see the pain I was inflicting on others as I shed my own. I told them how we get so caught up in what our Christian walks should look like that we forget that we are a hurting people in desperate need of a Savior.

Transparency

The words just tumbled out effortlessly, as God led the way. By the time I had finished, I was shaking and spent. I berated myself for thinking that I, as probably one of the youngest Christians in the room, had any right to talk about the Christian walk and judging others. I was still figuring things out myself and making plenty of mistakes along the way. More than that, since I wasn't really sure of all that I had said, I wracked my memory trying to think if I had said anything offensive that could have dishonored God. I was sure that I would never be invited back to another retreat. I doubted if I could even show my face in church.

As my mind raced wildly with all of these thoughts, the facilitator's voice snapped me back to attention.

"I feel that there is someone else that needs to speak tonight, someone who did not sign up on the list," she said. "The Holy Spirit is pressing upon me that someone else needs to share their heart with us." As she said these words, a young girl stood up and walked over to the microphone.

With courage and conviction in her voice, she began. "Karen, when you said that you had a message for someone here tonight, I knew you were talking to me before you even said another word. No one knows this yet, but I was raped two days ago." She hesitated, opened her mouth to say something else, but broke down in tears instead.

Her mother and those seated in the front row rose and enveloped the girl in their own tears. As they stood together at the podium, the facilitator asked that the rest of us bow our heads and close our eyes. She then asked those of us who had been sexually abused to come up to the front.

Healing in the Hurting Places

Soon, almost half of the room stood up front. She directed those still seated to come up and lay hands on us and she began to pray.

After an hour and a half of praying, tears, and hugs, we began to disband and head back to our rooms for the night. The young girl spotted me in the crowd and made her way over to me. I hugged her and told her how sorry I was for her pain and for what had happened to her. She thanked me for giving her the courage to say something. I told her that it wasn't me she needed to thank, but God.

Later that night, I couldn't sleep so I got dressed and wandered over to the picnic area near our rooms. I could make out the figures of a number of other women from our group sitting there. They had also been unable to sleep. As we chatted about what had happened that night, we saw a large burly man with tattoos approaching us. Fearing that we had been talking too loud and woke him up, we quickly stopped talking.

"Are you that Christian group?" he asked. *Uh oh, here it comes,* we thought. We glanced at one another and then one of the women nodded her head.

"You know, I was in jail," he started. Somehow, none of us seemed surprised. "I pushed drugs, I stole, I didn't give a damn about nobody," he continued. "Then some preacher came to visit and started talking to us about Jesus. And my life has never been the same since."

His eyes moistened as he lowered his voice. "Would you ladies pray for me? I'm in need of finding some good Christian fellowship and a local church I can get plugged into."

"Sure," we replied as we laid hands on our brother in Christ. As he headed back to his hotel room, I thought about how the Spirit had moved mightily that night. How I had felt God's presence so strongly—and about all of the people who are hurting and in need of someone to talk to—someone to understand, someone who won't judge them, but who's willing to pray with them and point them back to Christ. How we can be so quick to judge, not truly knowing what lay in someone's heart.

Just as I struggled that day in the hotel room, I struggle now with what to say to you as the reader of this book. If you have been the victim of sexual abuse, I know the heartbreak and pain you feel. Your life will never be the same as it was before, but through Christ's healing, it can become an even better, redeemed life for His glory. Depending on where you are in the process, it may seem like you will never get to that point. You have dark days and then some good ones and every time there is a flicker of hope, it seems that you get dragged back down into the pit.

That is because we have an enemy afoot, wanting to keep us captive. *"Be self-controlled and alert. Your enemy the devil prowls around like a roaring lion looking for someone to devour"* (I Pet. 5:8 NIV). Sometimes, it may seem easier just to give in because all of your best efforts seem to have little effect.

Take hope, dear reader; these are just the tricks the enemy plays on your mind so you give up.

Always remember that:

You belong to God, my dear children. You have already won a victory over those people, because the Spirit who lives in you is greater than the spirit who lives in the world (I John 4:4 NLT).

Christ has already paid the price for our freedom and He longs to see us walk in it. I understand how you feel, because I've been where you are. I pray that this book gives you the courage to turn to

Healing in the Hurting Places

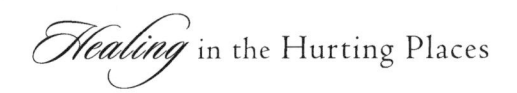

the only One who can heal your pain; I pray that you, too, will soon walk in freedom.

If you are someone who has not personally suffered sexual abuse, but who loves someone who has been affected, I know you are in pain, also. You want to see your loved one walk in freedom, but some days you might wish they weren't in your life because, no matter how hard you try to understand and help, it seems like you can't do anything right. It may be hard to hear that, but there is probably not a companion around who had not honestly thought that at one time or another. The road you are on is not an easy one, either.

There are times when their anger and hurt and frustration are directed at you and you aren't the cause. They might withdraw from you when you are trying to help or be in denial of what they are feeling. There are times when you can clearly see the enemy's attacks upon them, but you need to recognize that they might not.

They will heal on God's timetable, not yours. They may take one step forward and three steps back. Things may be good for weeks or months at a time and then suddenly, it's like you are back at square one. The frustration can almost be unbearable at times.

We must consider our own actions, as well. Sometimes as Christians, we think we need to keep a stiff outer appearance, that this is how we testify to the world that Christ is our Lord. But what He asks of us is transparency. We cannot speak into others' lives until they know we are real. This book is about breaking down those walls and admitting where we hurt and where our failures are, so we can begin to edify each other as the Body of Christ.

Chapter 14

Walking in Truth

Sometimes we do things because they are all that we have ever known. Other times we do things because we think they are the right things to do. Sometimes it is a little bit of both.

There came a point in my healing process where I felt like I was being stretched between two polar opposites. There were days and moments when things seemed fine and days and moments when I just couldn't get a grip on my emotions. I was caught in this back-and-forth cycle and it didn't seem to matter how much therapy, crying, praying, or time went by.

One night, I read to some of my friends some journaling I had done. They looked at me in shock. I didn't think it was that bad. But it wasn't the words that shocked them; it was the obvious message between the lines that I could not see.

One of them spoke to me boldly. "No wonder you are not healing," she said. "You can't stay in that situation and expect to heal."

Healing in the Hurting Places

I had never considered the alternative. My family of origin was all I had ever known since I was born. They were family. Good or bad, right or wrong, tough times and fun times—they were it. No family was perfect. Doesn't the Bible teach us to love and honor our mothers and fathers?

"But Karen, you are still sitting at the same table with your rapist. He hugs and kisses you in greeting like nothing ever happened. Your family knows what happened and thinks this is OK. This is not normal."

She had to be wrong. Christians forgave. Christians loved their brothers and sisters—all of them.

I had a lot to learn about the difference between legalism and walking in the light. And families are not only those by whom we are tied by blood. I thought it was important that I stay in the situation; that I be the salt and light. Aren't Christians called to be in the world, to reflect Christ to those who need to see it?

My friend persisted. "If it were your daughter, would you allow her to sit at the same dinner table as her rapist?"

I laughed. The thought was ludicrous. "Of course not," I said.

"Then why do you think less of yourself?" she questioned. "After all, you are the daughter of the King."

I was having trouble wrapping my head around all of this. Logic was colliding with tradition, truth with belief.

She could see my confusion. "Karen, think of it this way. You were small when it happened. It was not your fault. You were not responsible. But you are an adult now. You understand the difference between right and wrong and you recognize that what happened was sin. God forgives sin, but He cannot look upon it. He doesn't ask you to live with sin. Forgive the man who raped you when it is in your heart to do so, but don't confuse forgiving with tolerating."

I was listening intently, but I wasn't convinced. She continued, "You know that pedophiles don't stop. You couldn't do anything about it when you were a child. But you can do something about it now. By staying in the situation, you are not effecting any change. It looks like you are condoning sin because you are not taking a stand against it. If he hurts another little girl, how will you explain this to Jesus when you see Him?"

I swallowed hard. I didn't want to explain this to Jesus. I never wanted to see anyone hurt. I certainly didn't want this on my conscience. But there is a big difference between head knowledge and heart knowledge. And I really needed to be sure that I was doing the right thing before I made another move.

So I sought out God in prayer about this and I turned to the Scriptures. In Matthew, Jesus warns of division in households in His name:

Now brother will deliver up brother to death, and a father his child; and children will rise up against parents and cause them to be put to death. And you will be hated by all for My name's sake... (Matthew 10:21-22).

OK, so this helped me reconcile the fifth commandment about honoring thy mother and thy father. Honoring Jesus was foremost and took precedence over all. But wasn't Jesus the Prince of Peace? How could such division be allowed? I continued to read:

Do not think that I came to bring peace on earth. I did not come to bring peace but a sword. For I have come to "set a man against his father, a daughter against her mother, and a daughter-in-law against her mother-

Healing in the Hurting Places

in-law"; and "a man's enemies will be those of his own household." He who loves father or mother more than Me is not worthy of Me. And he who loves son or daughter more than Me is not worthy of Me. And he who does not take his cross and follow after Me is not worthy of Me. He who finds his life will lose it, and he who loses his life for My sake will find it (Matthew 10:34-39).

I began to take strength in Jesus' words. He went through many trials and was often misunderstood by His own friends and people. He lived much of His life as an outcast and was mocked and whipped before His crucifixion, for crimes He did not commit. He was and is the Prince of Peace. He came to free those who are enslaved and allow them to abide in His peace.

Paul struggled with his own personal trials and pleaded his case to the Lord:

And lest I should be exalted above measure by the abundance of the revelations, a thorn in the flesh was given to me, a messenger of Satan to buffet me, lest I be exalted above measure. Concerning this thing I pleaded with the Lord three times that it might depart from me. And He said to me, "My grace is sufficient for you, for My strength is made perfect in weakness." Therefore most gladly I will rather boast in my infirmities, that the power of Christ may rest upon me. Therefore I take pleasure in infirmities, in reproaches, in needs, in persecutions, in distresses, for Christ's sake. For when I am weak, then I am strong (2 Corinthians 12:7-10).

It seemed like the more I read, the more God's Word filled and strengthened me and gave me comfort. The books Paul wrote are filled with ways of dealing with difficult situations. The guidance comes from a man who understood situations, having been shipwrecked four times, whipped five times, imprisoned, stoned, and disbelieved. Yet, he kept his eyes on the prize, knowing that the trials he endured were a small price for knowing Christ.

While we know "Christian" is just another way of saying that we are "little Christs," striving to be like Jesus can be very daunting for a new Christian. That's why sometimes the examples of people like Paul and the apostles and even those in the Old Testament like David, Moses, and Abraham help show us the way when we think it is beyond our reach.

One of my main struggles was to understand the "Christian thing" to do in this situation. After all, I was mindful of my witness and the fact that sometimes, we are the only Bible someone else will open.

Then God directed me to Romans 12:9-21. My translation of the Bible entitles this section: "Behave Like a Christian":

Let love be without hypocrisy. Abhor what is evil. Cling to what is good. Be kindly affectionate to one another with brotherly love, in honor giving preference to one another; not lagging in diligence, fervent in spirit, serving the Lord; rejoicing in hope, patient in tribulation, continuing steadfastly in prayer; distributing to the needs of the saints, given to hospitality. Bless those who persecute you; bless and do not curse. Rejoice with those who rejoice, and weep with those who weep. Be of the same mind toward one another. Do not set your mind on high things, but associate with the humble. Do not be wise in your own opinion. Repay no one evil for evil. Have regard for good things in the sight of all men. If it is possible, as much as depends on you, live peaceably with all men. Beloved, do not avenge yourselves, but rather give place to wrath; for it is written, "Vengeance is Mine, I will repay," says the Lord. Therefore "If your enemy is hungry, feed him; if he is thirsty, give him a drink; for in so doing you will heap coals of fire on his head." Do not be overcome by evil, but overcome evil with good (Romans 12:9-21).

Healing in the Hurting Places

I decided that I would speak to my family in truth and love, and would ask God to help me with the words that I should use. We all have choices to make and they opted not to hear what I said and not to be willing to respect my feelings and need to heal.

And although it hurt greatly, I was comforted by the words of Jesus:

And when you go into a household, greet it. If the household is worthy, let your peace come upon it. But if it is not worthy, let your peace return to you. And whoever will not receive you nor hear your words, when you depart from that house or city, shake off the dust from your feet. Assuredly, I say to you, it will be more tolerable for the land of Sodom and Gomorrah in the day of judgment than for that city! (Matthew 10:12-15)

I am not going to tell you that this was easy or that I didn't question my decision. But I knew that my decision was based upon what I believed to be Jesus' truth. My family had a choice and they chose the rapist over their daughter.

Some people may find this hard to believe or understand, but I think I can. They did not want their world rocked. They wanted things to stay status quo, to pretend that the evil did not exist. I could not do that. It was not only for myself; it was for everyone.

If someone else had been hurt in that household as I was and I did not stand up to the evil, they might never find the courage to speak out, after seeing what happened to me. But by taking a stand, I was providing a safety zone for them, a place that they could come and be safe and not be alone—a place where they knew that someone would understand. So I needed to do this for them as much as for me. To give a voice to those who may not have found theirs yet.

The first Thanksgiving and Christmas, and my first birthday without my family was very painful, I will admit. I felt like an orphan, only my family had not died; they had chosen to turn away. Then I remembered Jesus' words and I found comfort:

> *If the world hates you, remember that it hated Me first. The world would love you as one of its own if you belonged to it, but you are no longer part of the world. I chose you to come out of the world, so it hates you. Do you remember what I told you? "A slave is not greater than the master." Since they persecuted Me, naturally they will persecute you. And if they had listened to Me, they would listen to you. They will do all this to you because of Me, for they have rejected the One who sent Me. They would not be guilty if I had not come and spoken to them. But now they have no excuse for their sin* (John 15:18-22 NLT).

Walking in God's Truth is not always easy. And we are not always going to stay on the right path, even when our intentions are good, because we are still learning. But David, an adulterer and a murderer, was known as someone who "chased after God's heart." It was from his lineage that our Savior came.

Our God is a God of forgiveness. He knows that we are going to trip and fall. He is there to pick us up, every time we fall. I can testify to this, because I have tripped up many times.

It's funny, when I was in grammar school, I was chosen as one of the narrators of the Stations of the Cross, which follow Christ's final journey to His death and resurrection. Year after year, although it was done in random order, I always got assigned to "Jesus falls for the second time." As a child, that station always confused me. Here is the Son of God and He is falling. God can do anything; I thought in my childlike mind, *How could a cross defeat Him?*

Satan thought the cross would defeat Him, but he was wrong. Although God, Jesus became Man in one of the great mysteries of life and assumed man's attributes. He became tired, He became hungry,

Healing in the Hurting Places

and yes, He even fell. While we can logically say this was due to the weight of the cross, being carried by a Man who had just been badly scourged, I can't help but think of the symbolism: God wants us to know that we all fall and, like Christ, we can get up again and defeat satan, through His strength.

I think it wasn't a coincidence that I was assigned to read that Station of the Cross year after year. I think God wanted it to serve as a reminder to me that it is OK to fall and that He in us will rise again.

And so, in Him I carried on. And in time, the peace that Christ promised did return to me.

Chapter 15

Eating Disorders

Like many victims, I have had a love-hate relationship with food. When I was growing up, I was told, "Have some dessert, it will make you feel better." Truth be told, it did. My favorite junk food was chocolate—candy bars, chocolate chip cookies, and chocolate ice cream with chocolate sprinkles.

Studies show that chocolate, particularly dark chocolate and those containing higher amounts of cocoa, contain polyphenols, also known as antioxidants, which benefit your cardiovascular system. "It also contains anandamide...caffeine, cannabinoids, tryptophan, and theobromine, all mood improvers. Chocolate also enhances the release of endomorphins and serotonin"[1] in the brain, which makes you feel better.

So there was definitely something physical going on when I put that candy bar in my mouth to make myself feel better. But now that I am learning to walk in God's truth, I know what was really going on was more emotional. I was looking for those "feel-good chemicals" to make me feel better emotionally, so the good feelings would hopefully

Healing in the Hurting Places

overtake any of the bad ones I felt. Food became a substitute for the love and attention I craved but did not receive.

In a way, it is not unlike the substance abuser taking another drink or putting another needle in his arm or pill into her mouth. At first, there is the rush of chemicals that alter feelings. And if taken in large enough amounts, the resulting images or feelings overtake the negative ones. I've heard drug abusers say that they'll take enough drugs to make them "feel better," while alcoholics often drink to forget the unpleasant memories that surface.

The irony of this is that the need to take nourishment into our bodies is a God-given instinct, just like procreation. Eating and drinking are hardwired into us. This makes eating disorders more of a challenge. A chain-smoker can quit cigarettes and never need to see them again, but we need to find a way to manage eating disorders, because we can't cut food out of our lives.

As babies, some of us were breast-fed and felt the closeness of our mother's body and heartbeat as we received nourishment. Even if you were bottle-fed, chances are when you were an infant, you were held close as you were fed. These memories were impressed on our brains and when we feel anxious, something deep inside us longs to create that feeling of being held close and secure.

For nine months, we grew and developed inside our mothers, felt their blood pumping through us, heard their heartbeats and their voices. Prematurely-born babies who are touched or held gain weight faster and thrive over babies who are not touched.[2] The power of touch never leaves us; similar results as to thriving and barely surviving have been reported in nursing home patients. Nurses and doctors recognize the healing power of touch.

Eating Disorders

Food can sometimes take the place of touch in our minds as a means of comfort and security. Sexual abuse victims have learned the negative aspects of touch. Since they may shrink back from being touched by anyone, food can become a substitute for touch in their lives.

Sexual abuse victims may also feel betrayed by their bodies. Their bodies may have responded biologically to the pleasure of being touched in private areas, while inwardly, they disdained the act. They may also have been hurt while the act occurred, so pain may have mixed with pleasure. This confusion often gets translated to food; whereas eating can cause us to feel good, we disdain the weight gain or appearance. Food, like touch, can become a source of pain or punishment.

The natural urges designed for survival go haywire when childhood traumas occur and are often later misused to satisfy the longing for comfort and security. For example, while chocolate may provide some benefits, overindulging in these high calorie, empty-nutrient snacks can become a problem, especially if managing weight is a concern.

Many sexual abuse victims suffer from eating disorders. They may be overweight, anorexic, or bulimic. Food is either a source of comfort or a means of punishment. This is where it becomes a vicious cycle. Food can become the victim's enemy as eating disorders make them feel worse about themselves, causing them to further seek or avoid food.

When you are overweight, others treat you differently and may even ignore you. I have experienced weight swings throughout my life and have definitely noticed that people respond differently when you are heavy versus when you are slender. This partly stems from modern society's obsession with looks and the "thin is in" standard (witness the rail-thin models in vogue today).

Healing in the Hurting Places

When singles are asked to rate the top qualities they look for in those they date, attractiveness consistently ranks in the top five for both men and women. There are many reasons for this. Again, the origin comes from our Creator and society has run with the idea. When you look at the animal species, the male is usually more brightly colored and will often flaunt these features in an attempt to attract the female.

Muscular, toned, airbrushed male and female models grace the covers of magazines in our supermarkets. Overweight models are relegated to cards in gag stores. Plastic surgeries for liposuction, fuller lips, breast augmentation, and more are on the rise, as are gastric bypass surgeries that reduce the size of the stomach and limit food intake.

Another reason overweight people are treated differently involves the outward messages they project to those around them. They may carry themselves poorly or dress in unflattering or baggy clothes to hide their size. Overweight women often wear little or no makeup—either in an attempt to make themselves less visible or because they don't care about themselves. All of these visual messages are broadcast loudly.

So those who are "super-sized" are perceived—perhaps subconsciously—as being out-of-control or not having a regard for their appearances. This is actually the closest to the truth. One of the main reasons that victims have food issues is the need for control. Being abused at an earlier age means that control over their bodies was taken from them; exerting control over food is one means of taking back that lost control.

They may have been told that they were attractive prior to or during the violation, and in their minds, removing their attractiveness is a means to prevent further abuse. Many victims have admitted to overeating so that potential suitors will avoid them. The hope is to remove the possibility of being abused again. The problem with this thinking, however, is twofold: Studies have *not* shown that perpetrators choose their victims based on attractiveness. Rape is a crime of rage and control, not passion. Secondly, rape victims are not disproportionably thin, again, because looks are not the deciding factor when choosing a victim.

Added weight can make the victim feel more secure, even if it is false security. Many consider it "insulation"; society as a whole shuns larger body types, so they avoid stares and unwanted attention this way. In a more concrete way, the layers of fat symbolically serve as a wall, separating them from the outside world and keeping their feelings and pain locked inside.

A greater reason for overweight issues thriving among the abused is the perpetuation of satan's lies. As he continually whispers in the victims' ears that they are nothing, worthless, unwanted, and unloved—the added weight reinforces this image. However, none of us want to feel unloved deep down. Therefore, this unwanted point of view sends us back to the refrigerator or pantry for more comfort food. The vicious cycle is complete.

Anorexics and bulimics also have a poor body image, but use starvation and excess exercise as a means to punish themselves for looking and feeling this way. They typically report hating their bodies and seeing themselves as fat when they look in the mirror, even when they are of average or below-average weight. It is easy for anorexics and bulimics to believe the evil one's lies. Just like those who overeat, those who purge are looking for control over their bodies.

While overweight people often see fat as protection against future assaults, those who binge and purge or starve themselves often do so to punish themselves for being attractive and causing the assault in the first place.

Healing in the Hurting Places

Bulimia nervosa was first diagnosed in the 1980s and is marked by two cycles: a binge cycle, during which the person consumes large quantities of food, followed by a purge cycle in which the sufferer forces himself or herself to throw up. Use of laxatives and diuretics, often accompanied by excess exercising, also marks the cycle.

If left untreated, bulimia can lead to tooth loss (from stomach acids eroding the tooth enamel during vomiting sessions), ulcers and ruptures of the digestive tract, electrolyte imbalance and cardiac issues including heart attacks and dehydration. Bulimia affects both males and females, commonly during the high school and college years.

Anorexia nervosa, on the other hand, targets more females and typically begins around the onset of puberty. Anorexics do not purge or eat large amounts of food. This disorder is marked by starvation, excess exercise, and often the use of laxatives. Anorexia can cause brittle skin, loss of the menstrual cycle, irregular heartbeat, stunted growth, bone loss, and shortness of breath.

All of these disorders can result in death if not properly addressed.

At the roots of all of these disorders is self-loathing—feelings of being dirty, ashamed, or embarrassed by some event or trauma.

Therefore, breaking the cycle is not as simple as putting down the fork, convincing someone that they are not fat, or trying to stop someone from purging. Unless the root of the problem is resolved, the behaviors will continue. Often, intervention is needed if the disorder is advanced. Even seemingly successful treatments often end in relapse. That is because the problem is deeper than the actual eating and exercise habits.

For myself, I was grateful for the isolation and inattention that my extra weight provided. Hating myself went hand-in-hand with hating how I looked. Receiving confirmation of this from others (who

Eating Disorders

ignored me, looked at me in disgust, or felt I lacked self-control) just served to support my worst fears.

Changing these behaviors involves more than just self-control, which is why most diets fail. In order to break the cycle of eating disorders, the person must begin to view themselves differently. They must learn to value themselves and see themselves as children of God who are wanted, loved, and created by Him. They must realize that their bodies are temples of God.

This is not an easy process. Satan's lies can be firmly entrenched in the minds of those who were abused. The reason for this is sin. Once sin has impacted our lives, the far-reaching effects are devastating.

This is why God warns us to avoid sin at all costs. It is not just because God hates sin; it is because He knows the havoc it wreaks upon the sinner and those impacted by the sinner.

King David is just one of the many biblical examples of this principle. One evening from his rooftop, he saw a beautiful young woman named Bathsheba taking a bath and decided that he had to have her. When David learned that he had impregnated her, he sent for her husband, Uriah the Hittite, to return from battle and be with her, so it would appear that the child was his. But Uriah was an honorable man and did not feel it proper to return to his home while the other soldiers were still in battle, so he did not go to his wife. Unable to cover Bathsheba's illicit pregnancy and his role in it, David sent orders to have Uriah killed in battle. (See Second Samuel, chapter 11.)

In Second Samuel 12, Nathan told David a parable in the hopes of opening the king's eyes to the sins he had committed. Instead of being remorseful, David became prideful and did not initially recognize himself in the parable.

Healing in the Hurting Places

Although David did finally repent and God forgave him, his sins had far-reaching consequences: the son David and Bathsheba conceived in adultery died shortly after he was born.

More tragedy befell David's family when his son, Amnon, sexually violated his half sister, Tamar. David's son, Absalom, then murdered Amnon in retaliation for the wrong done to his sister. (See Second Samuel, chapter 13.)

In Second Samuel 15, Absalom committed treason and in chapter 18 he was killed in battle, but not before fulfilling the prophecy that Nathan bore: What David had done in secret, Absalom did in public on the rooftops with David's concubines. (See Second Samuel 16:22.)

Sin does not only affect the offending party, it often impacts the innocent people surrounding the sinner. In David's case, Uriah, Tamar, and others suffered the fallout of his sin. In the case of childhood sexual abuse, the sin of the abuser impacts the victim and creates a domino effect that taints the lives of those around the victim, whether through a continuing cycle of abuse or the toxicity produced when the original pain is taken out on others.

Let's examine more closely the ripple effects of pain as seen in King David's family. Consider first the impact that Amnon's sin had on the feelings and actions of others, particularly Absalom and Tamar:

> *Then Amnon hated her exceedingly, so that the hatred with which he hated her was greater than the love with which he had loved her. And Amnon said to her, "Arise, be gone!" So she said to him, "No, indeed! This evil of sending me away is worse than the other that you did to me." But he would not listen to her. Then he called his servant who attended him, and said, "Here! Put this woman out, away from me, and bolt the door behind her." Now she had on a robe of many colors, for the king's virgin daughters wore such apparel. And his servant put her out and bolted the*

door behind her. Then Tamar put ashes on her head, and tore her robe of many colors that was on her, and laid her hand on her head and went away crying bitterly. And Absalom her brother said to her, "Has Amnon your brother been with you? But now hold your peace, my sister. He is your brother; do not take this thing to heart." So Tamar remained desolate in her brother Absalom's house. But when King David heard of all these things, he was very angry. And Absalom spoke to his brother Amnon neither good nor bad. For Absalom hated Amnon, because he had forced his sister Tamar (2 Samuel 13:15-22).

This story is not unlike those that occur today. Here we see Tamar, wracked with shame and her brother telling her not to take it to heart. Many abuse victims are told to "get over it," "it happened a long time ago, you must put it behind you," or "you need to move on with your life—thinking about this will not help."

Absalom is filled with rage (a common reaction when one hears of the abuse of another) and plots to kill his half brother. King David does nothing to punish Amnon. Some Bible scholars believe it is because Amnon was David's firstborn and was expected to succeed him on the throne.

Caught between Absalom's anger and David's ignorance, Tamar is left to suffer her shame and pain alone and in silence. She tears her robe of many colors, worn by the king's virginal daughters. At the time of this story, putting ashes on one's head and the tearing of the robe were signs of grief and mourning. Tamar had not only lost her virginity, but her prospects for marriage and a family.

In today's American society, the traditions of virginal marriages and prearranged weddings are nearly extinct. As singles choose their own spouses, other determining factors come into play, with physical attractiveness high on the list. The modern-day Tamar manifests the

Healing in the Hurting Places

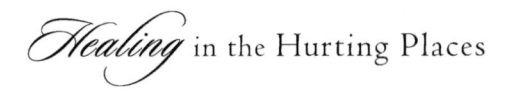

pain and shame she feels through her outward appearance as well, but this time using eating disorders as the means to express herself.

ENDNOTES

1. Cal Orey, "Nurses: Discover the Healing Powers of Chocolate," Working Nurse, https://www.workingnurse.com/articles/Nurses-Discover-the-Healing-Powers-of-Chocolate, accessed July 5, 2010.

2. Mark Tyrrell, "Premature Babies and Touch," Uncommon Knowledge, http://www.uncommon-knowledge.co.uk/touch/touch-2.html, accessed July 5, 2010.

Chapter 16

Yours in Healing

As time went on, I became more and more frustrated with how long the healing process was taking and why things in my life would not settle down. I just wanted everything to be OK again. What I couldn't wrap my head around at the time was the reality that things would never be the same again.

And that's a good thing. God has a much better plan for our lives than we could ever fathom. While change can be hard and uncomfortable, it can herald a whole new perspective and new ways of acting and being. I'm now learning to embrace change. That doesn't mean I always like and welcome it; it just means that I'm learning to trust and lean on God more.

If we always think we know what is best for us, then we aren't willing to let God be in control and we doubt that His plan is best. That's a very convicting thought for me. And it's something that I pray I will keep in mind when adversity strikes.

These are things I have learned coming out on the other side. I had to get there first. And to do so, God put a lot of people and situations in my life to shape and change my thinking. The main problem I faced was my sense that no one seemed to "get it." So one night, while surfing the Internet, I came across an online support group for survivors of childhood sexual abuse. It was an anonymous way to connect with trained counselors who were victims themselves.

The best part about it was that it was available any time. If I couldn't sleep at 2 A.M., I could log on and voice my pain and someone would respond. But the beauty of God's design is that in His economy, a single situation can benefit more than one party. The first time I logged on, a support member named Mike responded. We continued emailing for months, and as I went through the healing process, I believe he was blessed and encouraged as well.

Healing, One on One

Below are some excerpts from my months-long exchange with Mike. If you are a victim, you may hear yourself in the pain expressed here and discover that you are not alone in your feelings.

If you have not gone through this, it is my fervent hope that these excerpts will help you begin to understand what the victim you care about is cycling through and how you might be able to help him or her.

> To Whom It May Concern:
>
> I am a victim of childhood sexual abuse. I thought I was doing pretty well, but now I feel like I have just hit rock bottom and don't know where to turn. In praying about it, I discovered your support group online and hope that you

Yours in Healing

can help me. Thank you for your time; I look forward to your response.

Karen

Karen, believe me, you are similar to many others who join us as far as hitting "rock bottom" before seeking us out. I was the same way. Nevertheless you did reach out—an important point for you to always remember. You are not alone. Here you'll find out that, sadly, there are many others like you. In fact you'll discover that there are many things about you, and your pain and struggles that are not so different from all the other survivors. You are definitely not alone.

Nobody else, no matter how understanding and empathetic, "gets it" like someone else who's been through similar experiences as a child. I can tell you from experience that the first time I said out loud and in front of others that "I am an incest survivor," it was a feeling such as I'd never known. To be able to actually say that without fear of being judged, and without all the shame and guilt I'd carried for so long was a very good feeling. I've witnessed the same thing happen for others here. I hope you get to feel that as well.

One survivor said, "Incest is like screaming but hearing no echo." We try to provide those echoes.

Yours in healing,

Mike

Healing in the Hurting Places

Mike, thank you so much for being out there for me. It's like a lifeline that I so sorely need at this point. It helps me to know that you are out there and I am not exactly doing this all on my own.

I am really hurting now and that's hard to admit. "Hearing" the compassion in your emails is huge to me. This may seem silly, but I want a "time-out" to heal, to be nurtured, to be comforted, to be understood. I need a break from the hard work and lessons (i.e. growth). I am grateful that I have been forced to do some growing these past few months, but there is a point where this can tip too much to the other side and I'm on the end of the seesaw right now where I need a break. I took my first vacation in almost ten years just a few weeks ago and just went to the beach every day, walked along the surf, wiggled my toes in the sand and I can't begin to tell you how that helped.

But now I am back in the real world, with real-life decisions and reflections and quite frankly, I don't like everything about me. Especially the parts that are leftover self-defense mechanisms. The parts of me that drive others away because I don't feel lovable and if I push people away, then it becomes a self-fulfilling prophecy. The parts of me that are sinful, obsessive, prideful, selfish and a host of other things that I recognize as just acting out, but try as I might, I can't get a grip on them. The parts of me that have regrets and I know I can't change the past, but I want to heal so badly—myself, the relationships I have trashed, people I have hurt—and yet I know I am powerless over it all, the only thing I can change is me. So I'm *sorta on this stressed-out, pressure-filled roller coaster of emotions, anxiety, pain, and impatience right now.*

Whew! I am so sorry that all of that spewed out. I didn't mean to pour that out; I only wanted to say thank you for giving me the courage to say all of this.

Karen

Karen,

I didn't give you courage. Neither did I give you hope, or belief in the possibilities of healing. All I did was open the window to the courage, hope, and belief that you already had inside.

It's easier, as you probably know, to just think that you're really worthless at the core, and believe that if others ever discover your secrets they'll leave.

I too resisted admitting the seriousness of the consequences of the incest. I took the approach that I could read all the books, follow all the advice, and deal with it alone. I didn't see a need for talking with anyone. After all I was a smart guy, and, well, I could just "reason" my way through it. Didn't work out that way.

Without therapy, and certainly without my friends, I don't know where I'd be. Well, actually, I do know where I'd be—dead. I would not have made it. The fellowship with others who "get it" has been important to me. I'm not afraid to cry. And I'm not afraid when someone else cries. I'm not afraid to admit that it hurts—and why it hurts. I'm just not afraid, which is different from the way I've always lived. I was always afraid people would know, or find out

Healing in the Hurting Places

about me. Find out how worthless I was. Find out I'd just been pretending to be normal.

Yours in healing,

Mike

Mike,

Just got home from an in-person support group that I found. It was a great group of people and it was good to hear people that have felt (or are feeling) the same as I. Gained some insight as to why I have reacted/done certain things. I'm definitely going back and giving it a shot. I guess it was because I felt safe...and understood, for perhaps the first time.

OK, that's the good stuff. But I think you really wanted honesty. There's a part of me wondering what the future holds. When people have been struggling for 10 or 20 years and still have some of the same issues that I have—I'm left wondering—does it get any better or is this is as good as it gets? I've accepted the fact that I have been scarred by these experiences and nothing will ever change that. But it's scary to hear people that have been dealing with this longer than I sound like the same things can trigger them off, cause them to react, still have certain feelings. I know everyone's experience is different—and please understand, I didn't go to the group expecting a magical cure-all or anything.

But does it really get better? Or do I just accept that I will never, ever be normal? That for the rest of my life, I will always do things differently than other people and that I will drive people away, cause them to look at me differently or treat *me differently, because I am different. Is there ever a blending? What I mean is, can I hope that one day I might WANT to react a certain way because of my past, but my mind will have conquered that—and that past behavior will just be a distant memory and not a present truth?*

Is any of this making sense???

Karen

Karen,

Try to think of it like this...Somebody that loses an arm, or leg, or hand or something. Say, they were hit by a drunk driver. They will never be the same as if it had never happened. But that's not at all the same thing as saying they can never live a better life. Such a person will never be "normal," will they? But, they can still have friends; they can still have good careers. They can still laugh. They will still cry. And, they will still be angry about what happened.

Yea, I know, it wasn't the same for them as you and me. There was no betrayal. There was no intent to hurt. The drunk driver didn't do it to pleasure himself at their expense. And, most importantly, there was no need to torture themselves keeping "the dirty little secret." But, they'd still think some of the same things as we do. They'd have questions like "Why me?" or "What did I do to deserve this?" or "Why would anyone ever want to love me?"

Healing from this doesn't have an end point. Did you ever hear the saying about success not being a destination but a journey? It's like that for people such as us. Books, tapes, tears, fellow survivors, friends, spouses, children–those are all things that can

Healing in the Hurting Places

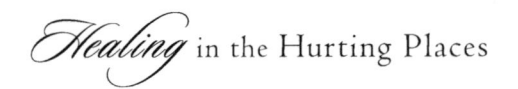

help us on the journey. But none of them will make it as if it never happened.

But Karen, you can take my word for it that if you start the journey, life can get better. Things do get easier. The memories get less intense. The pain gets less intense.

Remember, there's a part of you that fears people, believes they will hurt or rape you in some way all over again, and that since you are unlovable anyway it's best to drive them away before they do any of those things. Those fears fade quite a bit on the journey.

Eventually, you'll realize that conquering all this with your mind is only part of it. Only temporary. You'll need to use your heart as well. To forgive yourself. Forgive yourself for past transgressions, real or imagined. Your faith in God will help you with quite a bit, I'd say.

You already have a strong faith, and presumably already believe that God forgives you. But, you need to forgive yourself.

Haven't you already tried, and tried, and tried to conquer this with your mind? And it hasn't really worked out all that good, has it? Doing that, using your mind while ignoring the pain in your heart, well, is like using your credit cards to get all the stuff you need, but then the bill comes due.

Yours in healing,

Mike

Mike,

In group tonight, when I shared some things that were difficult, unusual, or self-indulgent; stuff that the "normal world" may cringe at or think inappropriate to say or feel, the others in the group just smiled, nodded, and even laughed with me. How empowering it was to know that others could actually understand the wide range of emotions I am experiencing and didn't censor them (as in telling me not to say or think that way, perhaps even quietly with their disapproving looks).

Perhaps—and this is a guess as well—that each time you retell your story or revisit those bad memories, it strengthens you against them. Is this right?

Karen

Karen,

Yes, that is right in ways I appreciate more and more all the time. I hope it will be that way for you as well. You and me, and all the others, well, we had no way to defend ourselves when we were children against the hurt, and the sadness, did we? But we're better able to do so now...

Yours in healing,

Mike

Mike,

I also want to tell you—and maybe this is still part of that "nurturing, want to fix it all and everyone else" syndrome—but my heart goes out to you and what you went through.

You allowed me to consider revisiting some of my own memories and how they played out and accepting that the consequences were not my fault.

Karen

Healing in the Hurting Places

Karen,

Good! That was the whole point in telling you! Well, that, and to encourage you to be more forgiving of yourself.

Yours in healing,

Mike

Mike,

I have tried—unsuccessfully—to deal with the actual abuse, forgetting that the fallout and aftermath are just as much a part of the scars.

Karen

Karen,

The fallout and aftermath are as much of the problem as the abuse itself, sometimes even more. Or at least that's what I believe. After all, if I really want healing, I am going to have to deal with it all at some point.

Yours in healing,

Mike

Mike,

One of my "faults," "vices," "issues," or whatever they are called, is to jump into something full speed ahead. If I'm not giving it 110 percent, I don't want to be in the battle. However, this time around—on this particular journey—I am trying to be "gentle to myself" and not push too hard. Just allow things to float around in my head and let my mind make sense of it when I am ready. So I am not going to try to understand or respond to it all—just settle for the little bits of wisdom as they come and take it slow. Taking it slow is a very radical concept for me.

But yes, you did point out what I have discovered over the past week—there is a huge disconnect between the head and the heart. I realized that when I read all of those self-help books last year and could spout it all back, but didn't "own" any of it yet. Not fully sure what the heart medicine is going to look like, but I'm sorta ready to take this step. I don't really have a choice. I don't want the life I had and I know the one I have now is better, and the best is yet to come.

Having you tell me that it gets better is incredibly encouraging. Whatever it takes, I'm committed to getting there. I know it won't be easy. But you give me confidence to believe that it will get better. You told me to take your word for it. Trust is still an issue for me, but because you shared your heart and your pain with me, I trust that it will.

Thank you so much!

Karen

You're welcome, Karen. Keep working at it. Keep going back to the meetings. You made me feel good with your email, and the kind words you wrote. I am glad to have been able, by happenstance and good fortune, to have helped you get started. It helps me keep going.

Yours in healing,

Mike

Healing in the Hurting Places

Mike,

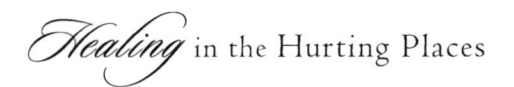

Well, it's been a week since I last logged on. I'm not depressed, I'm not withdrawn, I guess I'm just making time for me. Maybe I'm figuring out who me is. I know other people care—it's this wonderful, warm blanket drawn all around me, keeping me safe. But inside—well, it's just me and Jesus. I go to bed at night, holding His hand and asking Him to continue to keep me safe; walk me through this. As long as He's there, holding my hand, nothing else matters. That's just what I use to get me through the day.

Karen

Karen,

Glad to hear all's well. And yes, I think I understand where you are right now. And, if you don't mind my saying so, it's a good place for you to be. I'd guess there are things sorting themselves out in the background right now, without your even being aware of it, and as the days and weeks pass by you might just find some of those things have sorta faded away...

Yours in healing,

Mike

Mike,

I'm not sure anywhere is a good place for me to be right now. If I didn't have God in my life, I really think I would have committed suicide this afternoon. I'm just really, really not in a good place right now at all...

Karen

Yours in Healing

Karen,

In the last month or two you've glimpsed paradise for the first time ever. Even now I bet it's a tiny bit easier for you to understand what happened to you. You also have, albeit briefly, touched a freedom from your haunts and pain. The beauty of that freedom, and that paradise, is overpowering at first, and naturally stands out in very stark contrast to the ugliness of the abuse. Your eyes, and your thoughts, are drawn to the unimaginable difference between the two. It's not the ugliness of the past that draws your attention; it's the contrast between it and the future you've just glimpsed. A future, I might add, which is new to your thinking, and unexpectedly within your grasp.

The brunt of the storm your heart has borne would dim the deeds of a hundred men's lives. Don't despair that the clear skies following it are not yet fully overhead. You cannot by force of will, or bold determination, fight your way to clear skies. The clear sky will come to you. Which, I think, is the essence of your faith. Do your best to be ready for it.

Yours in healing,

Mike

Mike,

I feel like I just blew it. Things were starting to get better and now I'm back on this roller coaster again. I lost it with a friend of mine and blamed her for something that was my fault. She got so angry at me.

Healing in the Hurting Places

When I realized what I had done, I apologized and tried to explain that I am working on not taking things personally and reacting. But she said if I understood what I did was wrong, then I shouldn't have done it.

I can't tell you how upset and exasperated that made me. I wanted to scream at her—Don't you think I want to stop?!? Don't you realize that I'm more frustrated and fed up with all of this than you ever could be??? But now I look back at that as an empowering moment. I don't think for the rest of my life that I will get that look of anger in her eyes out of my head.

So…I have decided to finally get angry at the person who deserves it. I have spent my whole life protecting my family, caring what they thought and felt when they never gave a damn about me. Do you know since I told them what happened, they have never once brought it up, or asked how I feel or am doing?

So I have taken it out on the people around me that I care about—my husband, my kids, my friends. I was blaming them for something that they never had anything to do with.

Today I am going to write a letter and tell them exactly what this has done to me, how I feel. I am tired of tiptoeing around them and then taking my hurt and rage out on everyone else that had nothing to do with it. Is this going to hurt them and crumble their world? Probably. One of the reasons I have held off for so long. But so what? Do they care what it has done to mine?

Karen

Yours in Healing

Karen,

Nobody can truly understand how someone could do what was done to you. And to an even greater degree nobody else will ever understand how extensive the damage was to you. They all do understand, however, the effect its disclosure has on their lives. And so it is understandable that they wish it would all just go away.

Denial, from their perspective, is both possible and preferable. It may actually have benefits for them. You, and me, and all the rest of us, must always keep in mind that denial—from our perspective—is destructive. It may be possible for their understandable preference for denial to somehow blend with your equally understandable need for eliminating denial. But it may not be possible. Time will tell. Events will run their own course now, and there's little you can do to influence them. Stay true to your original purpose—HEALING!

Yours in healing,

Mike

Mike,

I have decided to start small. I took Jesus' hand last night and I let Him hold my hand while I fell asleep, to keep the nightmares away, to hold onto a dream of one day being happy again. And every night, I have held His hand. Some nights, I need to hold it tighter than other nights. Sometimes, He holds it very gently because He knows He can loosen His grip and I am not going to fear that the world will fall apart. Mainly, this

Healing in the Hurting Places

week, I have been learning to be gentle to myself. Not to care so much what others think or expect of me.

One night, I was supposed to help a friend by editing her work. In the past, I would have felt it was the right thing to do. It was expected. I owed her. It was being nice. It was being "good" and all the stuff I've told myself over the years to try to make myself feel good, but deep down, none of it really worked. So instead, I sat in front of the TV and when I felt tired, I went to bed. I am learning to be gentle to myself. I am learning to be true to my feelings. I am learning to care about me and let God love me. Someday, I may actually be happy again.

When I went to the meeting two nights ago, I shared this with them. I found acceptance and understanding. Some of the stuff I said prompted others. At first, we were sharing shameful, hurtful truths that we had buried. Soon, we were sharing crazy stories of nutty things we did to keep from hurting. And we began to laugh, we laughed so hard at each other and ourselves that tears almost flowed. At the end of the meeting, I thanked everyone. I told them when I joined I never thought that I could talk about the pain of incest and its scars—and laugh—all in the same hour. They understood exactly what I meant. It felt good—all of it.

Thank you for all of your encouragement. Without it, I may have never been able to take any of these steps. I appreciate how you keep checking in on me and making sure that I am O.K. I want you to be O.K., too. And for the first time, I am really believing that all of this is possible...

Karen

Yours in Healing

Karen,

This path to recovery we have all chosen definitely has ebbs and flows. Try to make good progress when it's flowing, and fight back as possible when it ebbs. No one can do more than that. No one can expect more than that of you.

Healing will come to you as you are prepared for it. The old Karen went about fixing things by taking action. This is different. You cannot speed or improve the process by force of will or decisiveness of action. Only the openness of your heart to recovery speeds the process.

We all spend lots of time and effort trying to understand why, as children and utterly defenseless, we were singled out for abuse. Who knows why? But you know what? You were also singled out for recovery. Think about that sometimes...

Yours in healing,

Mike

Mike,

It's been a very long week, but I'm doing much better now. I was listening to a praise and worship song about God reigning and I think that's appropriate for the week I've had. I'm so glad that He does reign and is in charge, not me.

You're right about the ebb and flow. The other night, it all caved in again. I was at a Bible study and I was surrounded by friends and people I know—people who care about me and I started thinking how we can't choose our families, but we can

Healing in the Hurting Places

choose our friends and how sometimes our friends become more like our families to us.

I thought about the people I've fought with this week, who got angry at me—and all of a sudden, the room began to swim. It was like people were talking in the room and they all sounded like they were underwater. Probably in hindsight, because I felt like I was drowning.

Suddenly, I just couldn't be in that room anymore. I felt like I was suffocating. It was all too much. I went outside into the cold, windy air and sucked the cold, dry air into my lungs like I was reviving myself, to no avail. I think I wanted to feel alive instead of just numb.

I sat in my car and stared up at the stars through the windshield and tried to decide if I blamed God for all that has happened and if I had a right to be angry at Him like my friend said. She accused me of doing what I thought Christians "should" do and not what my feelings told me. Don't get me wrong; I'm not letting anyone dictate how I feel—but I'm taking this all in and thinking about it and working so hard to get through it and while I could see the progress, at that moment in time, all I could feel was discouragement.

I leaned back and started thinking if I decided to kill myself, what method should I choose? I had never attempted hanging before. I started wondering what kind of rope I should use, what kind of knot—was it a slip knot?—and did I have any rope at home? Who would find me? How long would it take? Should I write a note? What would it say? Who would I write it to?

Yours in Healing

In the past, I've slit my wrists (more than once), walked out in traffic, almost jumped off a roof (I'm afraid of heights, so I never made it too close to the edge) and swallowed some pills. Hanging was a new one. I thought shooting myself would be way easier, but I didn't own a gun and anyway, with my aim, I'd be lucky if I didn't shoot my eye out. I knew deep down I wasn't serious, but man, I was thinking pretty hard about it.

I just sat there, looking at the stars and talking to God until the Bible study was over, as I was driving the carpool and couldn't leave. I went home, fell into bed in resignation and in the morning, prayed to God to give me an answer.

The next day, I ran into one of my friends. The first thing she said was how relaxed I seemed. I looked at her as if she had five heads. She then began to recite all of the progress she had noted in me and the positive results that she'd seen lately.

I silently thanked God for answering my prayer. Hope began to sprout again in my soul. As much as I wanted to see the positive, I couldn't find it anywhere. But it was there. She could see it for me and help me to see it, too.

It's all about the little things, how life can change in an instant. I was so discouraged until a friend came along with some words of encouragement. I know the progress is there, but it can get so damned tough to see it at times and all so overwhelming. I just found out today that a friend of ours whose four-year-old was in remission from leukemia had a relapse, and I realize I have nothing to complain about in life.

It's all so crazy at times, this thing called life, isn't it?

Karen

Healing in the Hurting Places

Karen,

Try to not think so much about everything. It's all out of your control anyway.

It's not your family you are breaking from. It's the circumstances and consequences of what happened to you as a child. That's what you're breaking away from. It is only the healing that matters now.

Yours in healing,

Mike

Mike,

I'm continuing to work on healing as I get a better grip on this and not let the circumstances color or alter my thinking. Also, I am moving away from some of the codependency behavior. I know I still have a long way to go and there are still times that I live moment by moment, but as I get a better grip on this and have more of a support system around me that either understands or is aware and trying to understand, it allows me to breathe easier.

This morning, I awoke with that image of Jesus holding the inner child of me safe from my abusive adult self and came to another realization. I recognize—as do other people—my manipulative/controlling behavior and expectations that I place on others, but another sin that is just as bad if not worse, that I have not identified previously, is justification.

Oh, others have pointed this out to me, but now I am beginning to see just how ridiculous I have been. I believe you even pointed me in this direction in one of your earliest emails. As a child, I justified my rapist's behavior because he has been sexually abused as a child; I went on to make more and more excuses as time went on. I even remember learning about human reproduction in biology class in high school and justifying his attacks as being due to him having too much testosterone! It would be laughable now if it wasn't so sad.

I realize how I have allowed myself to be used, taken advantage of, be a people pleaser, and when people treated me badly, I justified it. I valued them and their feelings more than my own. I decided that from now on—although it will be a learning curve—I intend to stand up for myself.

That I am beginning to wrap the serenity prayer around my heart more and more and I can only control from my heart to the end of my fingertips. When someone hurts me or negatively impacts me, I can state that and not try to justify it or avoid hurting their feelings. I can tell them that what they said was hurtful or upsetting or that I cannot deal with it right now or whatever.

What they choose to do with it is up to them. I will not manipulate or expect an apology or change in behavior and recognize that what they choose to do with the information is up to them and perhaps my stance may cause me to lose some relationships, but then they aren't the healthy relationships that I need to have in my life at this time.

I know it will take time to get better at this, but by learning to identify triggers, give myself time-outs, separate my emotions from rational thoughts and plan my words better before just spitting them out, I will move into this realm.

Healing in the Hurting Places

Another thing is that I had dinner with an old friend the other night. The first thing she noticed about me was, in her words, "that I have been taking care of myself." I think what she picked up on was more of the little things—I took time to put earrings in, my face had more color, I was carrying myself a little straighter, laughing a bit more, and more relaxed and less anxious. I was concerned less about what was going on around me and more about myself. It really made me feel good to know these small changes, day by day, are becoming evident to those around me.

Karen

Karen,

What was done to you had a prominent part in shaping you. And shaping you from a young age; as a girl, as a daughter, as a sister, and eventually as a mother and wife. Think about it. Every single relationship you've ever entered into since you were a child–business, casual, personal, etc.–was entered into by a Karen very different from today's Karen.

That Karen doesn't even exist anymore. All those people, every single one of 'em, had a relationship with her. Not with you. Not with the "you" that exists now. None of them have any idea how to have a relationship with you now. You're a different person now. (That's an understatement if ever there was one!)

Something very unsettling has come into their lives, completely unexpected, and they are all scrambling to figure out how to deal with it. That's understandable. Ya gotta accept that part of it. If you and I were in a situation like that we'd react, at least initially, in similar fashion. It's gonna take quite some time for them, and

Yours in Healing

their lives, to re-settle into something approaching normalcy. A new normalcy, perhaps.

For now they are all retreating to safe places. They all have a ton invested in the world in which they live, be it fantasy or real. They are unlikely to venture too far out of it.

What happened to you as a girl made you different from them. There is no denying that as fact (even though it wasn't your fault). But you were a different girl, and then a different teenager, and then a different woman. That girl, that teenager, that woman is the one they know. They don't know, and could never understand, the woman you are now becoming. And they probably never will.

Their shallowness is deplorable, and regrettable. But it is a fact. A hard fact, but true nevertheless. It hurts to have to accept that the family you actually have is not the family you thought you had. But that family is dead. It may never have even existed in the first place. Forget them. Forget, as best as you can, all of them.

But just as silence and denial enabled you to survive as a girl, acceptance and understanding will now enable you to live more fully than you could have otherwise lived.

There are others in your life who will help you, to varying degrees, as you work on understanding. And Jesus. They are with you. Look to them for life. For help. For comfort.

Yours in healing,

Mike

Mike,

I have to be totally honest with you. I truly appreciate all the wonderful things that you have said about the courage I have

Healing in the Hurting Places

given you and about traveling the very difficult and long road in an amazingly short time. But I cannot take one iota of credit for it. OK, just one—that I gave it to God. But I will boast in Jesus Christ—His death and resurrection.

If all the pain that I have been through in my life occurred so that you would one day find God and embrace Him, then I can honestly say it was worth every minute of it. Because my prayer for you is that someday, when you close your eyes at night and put your head on your pillow, you will not think of your past. You will see, feel, taste, and own—down to every fiber of your being and every pore of your body, the love the Father has for you.

Do not ever confuse it with the "love" in the way that your earthly father showed it to you. You see, Jesus wants to take away that pain, He truly does. He knows more than anyone, when He was betrayed by His friend, Judas—a man He ate with and walked with and taught with—what betrayal feels like. He knows when He was scourged repeatedly, the spiny whip ripping the skin from his torn and bleeding back over and over again, what real pain is. When He hung on that cross—having the power of God to remove Himself from it with only a word—what it was like to suffer.

This is what is healing me. It is not the power of the support group, or all the wonderful words you and others wrote me, it wasn't the books I read or the prayers I uttered. All of that helped and encouraged me. God sent all of that to me and used every bit of it to get me to the place I am now. But the only thing that could possibly heal me was finally breaking down and giving all that pain to the One who knows what pain is.

Yours in Healing

I know for me, that was Jesus. He was waiting in the wings the whole time, ready to sweep me up in His arms and acknowledge the pain and wrap me up in His true love. He truly knows the pain you have felt, that I have felt, what we have gone through. The Father has seen all of it and Jesus knows what it felt like.

I will pray that in His perfect timing, you will be healed. I want so badly to hand it to you, but I cannot. But I do know that it is there for you, for the asking.

Karen

Karen,

You wrote this to me a long time ago: "You've turned the pain of your past into a healing for others and perhaps one day, I can do that, too."

You already do that, Karen. You've done that for me each time you have reached out to me, trusted me with your pain, your confusion, your desperation, and especially as you shared each step forward you've accomplished. As you share your healing with me I gain more courage to continue mine. To me, that is the miracle. It's an honor to witness your healing while knowing how you suffered the way you have. Whether or not I played any part in it is totally irrelevant to me.

The beauty of your healing, of each step you take forward is stunning.

You've given me a lot of extra courage. You have traveled a difficult and very long road in an amazingly short time. Many survivors (me included) needed a much longer time to make the progress

Healing in the Hurting Places

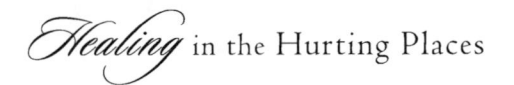

you've made. Truth be told, what you've done for your own healing and recovery is amazing, and would be so even if it took a year or more. Kudos to you...

Yours in healing,

Mike

Chapter 17

Fear of Success

Humans are filled with fear—fear of flying, fear of snakes, fear of failure. Our two greatest fears are of public speaking and death, in that order. Global and economic crises bombard us. The information superhighway overloads our senses. Our fears of nuclear war, terrorist attacks, and the end times as promised in Revelation become heightened.

The word *fear* appears 260 times in the Bible. And yet the prophet Isaiah exhorts us not to fear:

> *Say to those who are fearful-hearted, "Be strong, do not fear! Behold, your God will come with vengeance, with the recompense of God; He will come and save you." Then the eyes of the blind shall be opened, and the ears of the deaf shall be unstopped. Then the lame shall leap like a deer, and the tongue of the dumb sing. For waters shall burst forth in the wilderness, and streams in the desert. The parched ground shall become a pool, and the thirsty land springs of water; in the habitation of jackals, where each lay, there shall be grass with reeds and rushes. A highway shall be there, and a road, and it shall be called the Highway of Holiness. The unclean shall not*

Healing in the Hurting Places

pass over it, but it shall be for others. Whoever walks the road, although a fool, shall not go astray. No lion shall be there, nor shall any ravenous beast go up on it; it shall not be found there. But the redeemed shall walk there, and the ransomed of the LORD *shall return, and come to Zion with singing, with everlasting joy on their heads. They shall obtain joy and gladness, and sorrow and sighing shall flee away* (Isaiah 35:4-10).

Fear is something that held me captive for a long time. I was afraid to cry out when I was a child. Fear and shock kept me frozen and unable to react and process what was happening to me at that time.

I was afraid to speak out afterward; I was afraid of not being believed or worse, breaking up or being put out of my family. In school, I was afraid that if others knew what happened to me, I would be ostracized and bullied. The fact that I *was* ostracized and bullied only confirmed my worst doubts—everyone knew my story and I would be treated differently because of it.

Being a victim of abuse sets a dangerous cycle in motion: you act differently because of what happened to you and because You act differently, people do not treat you the same way they treat others. This reinforces the guilt, shame, and isolation the victim feels. As the victim withdraws, there are fewer people in their world to potentially help and encourage them.

Patterns develop and soon the only people victims attract are those waiting to take advantage of them. Often, others perpetuate the abuse. It may be the same kind, as in the child of an alcoholic marrying an alcoholic and then getting divorced and remarried to another alcoholic. It may be a different form of abuse: They may have been sexually abused as children and then marry into a situation where they are domestically abused by a spouse.

Because the victim either feels at this point that no one else will love them, or that they are unworthy of being loved and are therefore

Fear of Success

grateful that somebody *seemingly* loves them, the new abuse seems like such a small price to pay. They may even feel by this time that they deserve the abuse, having convinced themselves that they must have caused the initial abuse to occur.

It's hard to explain to someone who has never felt worthless what this is like. You stop caring and believing that anything good could—or worse, should—come your way. Like those with anorexia or bulimia, your mind has set you up to believe that you deserve whatever punishment you get. In a strange way, you almost welcome it, even though with every attack, blow or insult, you shrink a little deeper into the pit. It's almost like the child who misbehaves just to get attention, because any attention—even bad attention—is better than none at all.

There probably isn't a victim out there who doesn't want to survive and become a whole person again, at least on the surface. But the reality is that you become so used to how you have lived your whole life that it's scary to be on the other side. The unfamiliar is a very strange place indeed. It is new territory and that can be terrifying.

I remember thinking: *What do I do now? What do I say?* You would think you could just go about your life as before, only now the pain is not part of the equation. But it's not that easy.

I've seen this phenomenon over and over again. Alcoholics who quit the bottle struggle to enjoy a life without lies, excuses, and the world revolving around drink. There are criminals who have such a difficult time adjusting to life outside of prison that they commit petty crimes just to get back into jail.

It may not have been an ideal life, it may not have been pleasant, but it is the life you know. The bottom line is that none of us likes change or being out of our comfort zones. I have watched risk takers, such as those who like extreme sports, become paralyzed at the challenge of some mundane activity that most of us would yawn at. It's

Healing in the Hurting Places

not what the environment encompasses that proves frightening; it's a matter of not having experience with it.

Think about a bridegroom who gets "cold feet," or someone who has to speak for the first time before a large audience, or the knot you get in your stomach when the roller coaster climbs that first hill. If you got married, gave a speech, or rode a roller coaster on a daily basis, you would no longer feel that dread.

But it goes beyond the feelings of the person. That is just where it starts. I'm sure that some of those feelings get projected outward and others pick up on the vibes. The people around the healed or healing victim also need to adjust. They have gotten used to the victim's ways and have adapted themselves accordingly. It will take time to respond to the changes before them.

I remember this being one of the most frustrating parts as I neared the end of my journey. I felt like the moment I had awaited for most of my life had arrived and no one noticed. Not only did they not notice, but they still treated me the old way. Worse, some of them seemed to prefer the "old me."

The reality wasn't that they wanted me back the way I was. They were thankful to see the cloud lifting, to see peace filling my life. But it was unfamiliar terrain for them as well. Humans tend to choose the path of least resistance and that means falling back on what you know.

After Jesus died and the tomb was found empty, the apostles felt lost. They didn't continue their new lifestyle after Jesus was gone. With 12 of them, they could have easily banded together, encouraged one another, and tried to carry on. But they didn't do this until after Jesus appeared to them on Pentecost and filled them with the Holy Spirit (see Acts 2).

Initially, each fell back on the lifestyle he'd known before being called by Jesus. Why? Because it was familiar. The old life was as comfortable as an old sweatshirt or a broken-in pair of shoes.

When Jesus returned, He found Peter fishing. What did Jesus do? He didn't yell at Peter and condemn him for not continuing his walk of the past three years. No, instead, He met him where he was—fishing—and told him to cast his net on the other side of the boat.

When he did, Peter reeled in so many fish that it almost broke the net. It was not logical for Peter to put the net on the other side of the boat, but he did as Jesus suggested. And he saw much gain.

This is how we have to approach our new lives. We cannot simply leap into something entirely new and expect everyone to follow along. If God has put you in a certain place—be it an occupation or a lifestyle—there is a reason for it and growth is possible there. God doesn't expect radical change from us. Just like Jesus met Peter where he was at, we have to realize that people need time to adjust to the changes, just like we do.

So it may mean continuing what we were doing, only casting the net on the other side of the boat. Jesus knew Peter was a lifelong fisherman and, after Pentecost, Peter became a fisher of men. Jesus didn't turn him into a ruler or an electrician.

I remember when things began to really change for me and I got so caught up that I wanted to change everything. One area I had really struggled in was weight loss and I thought if God was changing me in other areas, this area would change radically, too. It did, but not overnight like I thought. I tried to force the issue by meeting with a Christian nutritionist and then going out to the store and buying everything on her recommended list.

Healing in the Hurting Places

There is a reason why it is called "recommended" and not "mandatory." But I was so determined to effect change in every area of my life that I blew past this. I also ignored the fact that the changes that had been occurring were due to Christ working in me, not my own hand leading the change.

Needless to say, I doomed myself to failure and this only made me feel worse. I began to question if I was even capable of anything. I had started to taste freedom—and it went to my head.

What went wrong? Well, the nutritionist had the best intentions at heart. Her recommended food plan was a good one. The problem was that it was not tailored to my likes, schedule, or lifestyle. I couldn't simply buy all of the foods on the list and think I would magically lose weight.

Problem number one is that I did not like all of the foods she suggested, and I never told her this. I thought I would just force myself to eat them and eventually like them. Or if not, I would adjust to eating them anyway. This is not realistic. This causes a person to feel frustrated and denied. It can lead to breaking the diet, embarking on food binges, or eating the wrong foods as a reward for suffering and doing the right thing. The point is: No one sticks for very long with something they feel was forced upon them.

Secondly, I jumped into my weight-loss mission with my old drive and single-minded focus. I didn't take into account the time needed for shopping, preparing the meals, and other tasks too time-consuming to be workable. I didn't stop to consider a realistic way to make my efforts effective.

Lastly, I wasn't gentle with myself, allowing time to adjust to this new lifestyle change. Often, we are much harder on ourselves than God could ever be. Jesus assures us that "*...My yoke is easy and My burden is light*" (Matt. 11:30 NASB).

Fear of Success

We do not have to take everything on ourselves and be difficult taskmasters. We can turn our burdens over to Him and let God lead the way. I am reminded of how the clay still fights against the potter's hand until the piece is finished. But as the pottery nears completion, the clay yields more and more to the potter's gentle touch. We need to do the same thing with our heavenly Father.

Part of my fear of success was that the enemy was always close by, ready to whisper in my ear about how I came so close, but did not quite do it. Our own thoughts and minds can be our worst enemies. But just as we become used to failure, we can become accustomed to success—success in Him. Sometimes we find our goals were never God's goals and it is better that those did not succeed.

It becomes a matter of faith. Those who trust in the Lord have nothing to fear from men. *"Fear of man will prove to be a snare, but whoever trusts in the LORD is kept safe"* (Prov. 29:25 NIV).

Jesus shared parables to teach men when He was on Earth. Consider these words:

While a large crowd was gathering and people were coming to Jesus from town after town, He told this parable: "A farmer went out to sow his seed. As he was scattering the seed, some fell along the path; it was trampled on, and the birds of the air ate it up. Some fell on rock, and when it came up, the plants withered because they had no moisture. Other seed fell among thorns, which grew up with it and choked the plants. Still other seed fell on good soil. It came up and yielded a crop, a hundred times more than was sown." When He said this, He called out, "He who has ears to hear, let him hear." His disciples asked Him what this parable meant. He said, "The knowledge of the secrets of the kingdom of God has been given to you, but to others I speak in parables, so that, 'though seeing, they may not see; though hearing, they may not understand.' This is the meaning of the parable: The seed is the word of God. Those along the path are the ones who hear, and then the devil comes and takes away the word from their hearts, so that they may not believe and be saved. Those on the rock are the ones who receive the word with joy when they hear it, but they have no root. They believe for a while, but in the time of testing they fall away. The seed that fell among thorns stands for those who hear, but as they go on their way they are choked by life's worries, riches and pleasures, and they do not mature. But the seed on good soil stands for those with a noble and good heart, who hear the word, retain it, and by persevering produce a crop. No one lights a lamp and hides it in a jar or puts it under a bed. Instead, he puts it on a stand, so that those who come in can see the light. For there is nothing hidden that will not be disclosed, and nothing concealed that will not be known or brought out into the open. Therefore consider carefully how you listen..." (Luke 8:4-18 NIV).

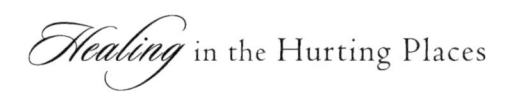

We are told that faith comes from hearing the Word of God. One of the best ways that I know to combat the fear of success is to immerse myself in the Word of God. As I read, God speaks to my heart and quells any anxiety. A verse that has been particularly reassuring to me is: *"For God has not given us a spirit of fear and timidity, but of power, love, and self-discipline"* (2 Tim. 1:7 NLT). The discipline of reading His Word every morning has helped me learn to trust and lean on Him for all provision. My fear, I learned, was really about a lack of trust and faith.

Then He got into the boat and His disciples followed Him. Without warning, a furious storm came up on the lake, so that the waves swept over the boat. But Jesus was sleeping. The disciples went and woke Him, saying, "Lord, save us! We're going to drown!" He replied, "You of little faith, why are you so afraid?" Then He got up and rebuked the winds and the waves, and it was completely calm. The men were amazed and asked, "What kind of man is this? Even the winds and the waves obey Him!" (Matthew 8:23-27 NIV)

Fear of Success

I have personally seen, as I turn over the reins of my life more and more to Him, how much easier the journey has become. We must accept that we cannot change others, but we can pray for their peace and for His will to be done in their lives, as we pray the same for ourselves.

We cannot become so focused on the outcome that we forget what He is doing in the details. His promises are always true and His Word does not return void. As He shows me this over and over again, the fear of success is no longer a concern. I am too enthralled in the journey.

God wants to be involved in all aspects of our lives. And I believe when we earnestly seek Him, He rewards and encourages us. I am always in awe when I sense His presence.

Recently, I was struggling to lift a heavy wheelchair from the trunk of my car. I wanted to help my friend out during a conference we were attending, but days of wrestling with the wheelchair were starting to wreak havoc on my back. At the end of the third day, I stood next to the trunk, exhausted and feeling unable to lift the chair one more time. I prayed for God to provide me the strength.

No sooner had I uttered that prayer, when a young man appeared by my side. "Do you want some help?" he offered.

Without thinking, I replied, "Well, it's heavy."

"No problem," he said. "I work for a medical supply company. I lift these every day." He quickly lifted the chair from the trunk and set it up on the ground. I have no idea where he came from as he was not attending the conference and we should have been the only ones at the facility. I helped my friend out of the car and turned to thank the kind young man, but he was gone. He had disappeared almost as quickly as he appeared.

Healing in the Hurting Places

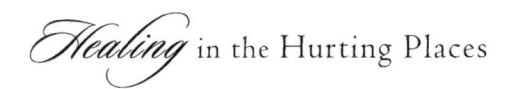

At one time, I would have believed the odds of a person showing up to assist with a wheelchair who actually did that kind of work for a living to be an amazing coincidence. I no longer believe these are coincidences.

Many times in my healing journey, I was sure that I knew all of the answers or how the situation should end up. It was easier to believe in the improbable or my own abilities. Moreover, I had a very short timetable for those results.

A joke I heard in church goes like this: "How do you make God laugh?" The answer: "Make plans." God has shown me over and over, by changing the ending, answering prayers on His timetable instead of mine, or blessing me when I least expected it, how silly it is to make plans. How much more freeing and empowering it is to rest on His wings.

> *But those who hope in the* Lord *will renew their strength. They will soar on wings like eagles; they will run and not grow weary, they will walk and not be faint* (Isaiah 40:31 NIV).

The fear of success is best silenced by resting in our faith.

Chapter 18

In Need of a Savior

I arrived at the park late. The speaker was just getting into the meat of his testimony about how he had tried all of the 12-step programs and other resources. His drug addiction landed him in the sanitarium twice. While in there, he promised his dad that when he got out, he would quit drugs for good.

Instead, he shot up the next day.

If you have been abused, if you have ever struggled with weight issues, substance abuse, or other problems that control your life, you will probably relate to his story.

If you have not had these issues, it may be hard for you to understand the grip they can have on a person. I want to say to you as an encouragement—you cannot love the person enough to get them to stop. They can't love themselves enough to stop. It's not your fault that they are hurting and there is little you can do to get them to end the behavior. They are not doing it to hurt you; although I'm sure that their actions do hurt you in many ways.

Healing in the Hurting Places

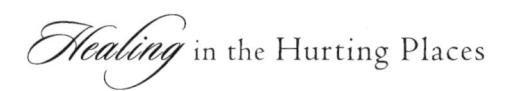

For the record, I am sure that I speak for most or all of us when I say that we've seen the pain in your eyes. We hear your frustration and quite frankly, it only makes us more frustrated. For the substance abuser, they may take that next drink or hit just to drown out the image of pain on your face. Please don't misunderstand; I am not blaming you or saying you are the problem or that this is your fault.

It's just that we are so disappointed—in ourselves, in our behavior, in the hurt that doesn't ever seem to want to go away. Knowing that we are causing another to hurt can be too much for us at times, because we do "get it." We know how you feel. The problem is that you can't know how we feel.

I recall a friend once saying to me when I was working through the meat of my issues and was angry all of the time, "If you're not angry at me, why are you taking it out on me? What else am I supposed to think? If you don't feel this way about me, stop doing it."

If it were only that simple. I remember hearing that and thinking, she will never understand. She just doesn't get it. Remember Mike, the one who befriended me on the support line? He explained it to me this way:

> It's so hard what we are trying to do. Hard for you, and me, and all the others like us. That's what I mostly think about. How hard it is. I don't think about it being unfair, or the perversity of it much at all now. I don't think near as much anymore that it's futile, or hopeless. And I don't get angry as much, or as intensely. I just think about how hard it is.
>
> I feel better when I say a prayer. I said an "Our Father" this morning. I said one yesterday too. Except I say "my Father" instead. Silly, isn't it?

In Need of a Savior

In answer to your question, this is what I think about the "regular people," the ones who haven't gone through what we have. I call them "reggies." Some of 'em I like a lot. Others I don't. Some of 'em like me, others don't. But mostly I think about how hard it is to do what we are doing.

How hard is it for the reggies, do you think? Not how hard is it for them to live their lives. How hard is it for them to interact with us? To care for us? I mean actually care for us as a person?

On really dark days it was easy for me to feel that they would hate me like I hated me if they really knew me inside. I was wrong when I thought that because I didn't actually know me inside either. I only knew what I was taught to see. There was more there and now I can see it better. So, I was wrong the way I looked at me.

I can see inside better now. But I can't see everything. I suppose I never will see everything. But for us, and the others like us, there's more places we have to look when we look inside.

Reggies have things they keep inside too. Not things like we do, but things nevertheless. They hurt sometimes. They are sad. They fail sometimes.

Comparing hurts, or sadness, or failures is pointless. We probably hurt more than they do. Our failures seem more serious to us. Sadness runs worse for us. But still it's a matter of degree. And they don't see so much difference between their hurts and our hurts. Maybe there's a lot more difference than even you and I think. Maybe there's not so much difference after all and we just think there is.

The biggest difference to me, as I see it, between us and reggies is how much deeper our hurts are buried. Our sadness. Our

Healing in the Hurting Places

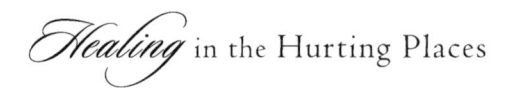

disappointment in our failures. I don't think any reggie gets that part. For them, once they decide to address an issue, or a hurt that's within themselves, it's not as hard for them because it's not buried as deeply as ours are. They just don't get how much work it is to dig that far down.

I don't think they'll ever get it. Sometimes they'll lose out by not understanding. They'll miss out on a good person because they don't understand. Sometimes it's us that loses out.

I know I'm different than my reggie friends. Even if they hurt the same as me. Or have the same amount of sadness as me. They can feel good easier than me. They have more moments of peace. Of joy. Of happiness. We have to work hard for those things. Joy doesn't come our way as often. So that's why I am different than reggies. We all are, I believe.

I have friends that love me. I do not doubt their love. But still I have to say to myself, they don't really know me. At least there are parts of me they don't know. The difficulty is that the very same parts they do not know, or will ever know, are not important to them (they love me with or without those parts). But to me those very same parts, the hurt and sadness, are foremost in my mind and heart constantly. So I guess there's always a friction about that.

It must be so horrible for you. There's the same friction between me and my friends and me as there is between you and your family and friends. But I see my friends for a couple hours at a time, once or twice a week. You see some of these reggies all day, every day. It must be so hard for you.

I don't have to pretend anymore. That's a good thing. And I am not afraid of my "secrets" anymore. That's a very good thing. As a boy I wanted to believe that if they all knew my secrets they'd love me anyway. That turned out to be true. I also longed for everyone to understand. That'll never be true. I've had to settle for the fact they know. But they'll never understand. I'm glad for them they don't, since it means it didn't happen to them. But it did happen to me. They'll just never understand what it's like. But I think I can live with that.

Support groups are wonderful. So are family and friends who care. All of them can and do help. The problem is that they are all human. People can only take so much, especially when they don't see results. I'm sure that I "burned out" a number of caring people in my life who just couldn't take it anymore. I know now that they loved me, but it all became too much for them.

One of the things that was important for me was consistency. I expected people to give up, to leave me—not because it was too much for them, but because I wasn't worth hanging in there for. That's how I felt at the time. So if someone stayed no matter what I did, that helped me to think that maybe I wasn't looking at things in the right way... that maybe there was something about me worth staying for.

But every time I gained hope, they reached the end of the line. Even when they didn't physically leave, they abandoned their efforts and created distance between us. This only convinced me more that my original thoughts were correct.

There are several problems with all of this. First, it is flawed thinking—it is a lie from the devil. Satan loves to grab onto random negative thoughts and twist them around in our minds until they appear to be truth.

It has been this way from the beginning of time.

In the Garden of Eden, God told Adam:

Healing in the Hurting Places

Of every tree of the garden you may freely eat; but of the tree of the knowledge of good and evil you shall not eat, for in the day that you eat of it you shall surely die (Genesis 2:16-17).

Eve had not been created yet. When she came on the scene, the serpent approached her and asked, *"Has God indeed said, 'You shall not eat of every tree of the garden'?"* (Gen. 3:1).

Eve replied:

We may eat the fruit of the trees of the garden, but of the fruit of the tree which is in the midst of the garden, God has said, "You shall not eat it, nor shall you touch it, lest you die" (Genesis 3:2-3).

Right away, we have a few problems. The original statement by God was made to Adam before Eve was created. We do not know if Eve ever heard that commandment directly from God later or if it was told to her by Adam. But she gave a slight embellishment to it, when she said "nor shall you touch it" as that was not part of what God said to Adam.

Being human, we have a tendency to hear what we want to hear. Many of us played the game "telephone" as children where one person whispers a message into someone's ear and they pass it on to the next person. When it gets back to the original person, it is generally far removed from the original message. Each person adds their personal interpretation to it.

The problem with this is that we can water down or even change the intent of the person who first made the statement. When we are hurt or in pain, we often listen from that place of pain.

Satan knows our weak spots. And if he can get us to believe his lies about those weak areas, he knows he has a good chance of making us fall. But here is the beautiful thing I have learned about falling—when

In Need of a Savior

we are down on our knees or even on our faces, we are in the perfect place of surrender to God. We are already in that low spot. As a pastor once told me, from that vantage point, all we can do is look up—into the face of the Savior who can help us.

Listen to how satan responded to Eve:

Then the serpent said to the woman, "You will surely not die. For God knows that in the day you eat of it your eyes will be opened, and you will be like God, knowing good and evil" (Genesis 3:4-5).

What is the first thing he did? He told her that she would not die. While many people today fear death, Eve may not have had a concept of what death was. But because she was created in God's image and was without sin up till that point, she had been living a blissful life walking with her Creator in The Garden.

Sin and death without salvation separate us from our Creator. So I suspect that on some level, her soul feared that possibility, even though she may not have cognitively understood it, because God knew what was going to happen before He created the foundations of the earth.

So satan refutes what God has said. Don't we do the same thing when we question whether God has really told us something, simply because we don't like the answer? I know there have been times for me personally when I unquestionably knew the direction God had for me. He made it very clear. But since I didn't like the answer; I questioned whether I really heard from God, even though my heart knew the truth.

Once doubt has been planted, satan attacks the weak spot. He tells Eve that her eyes will be opened, that she will be like God, knowing good and evil. How many of us want our eyes opened? Don't we make comments like wishing we had a crystal ball? Horoscopes, psychics, and fortune tellers wouldn't abound if people weren't seeking to know things that have not been revealed to them.

Eve's pride—or desire to better herself—resulted in the first sin of disobedience to God. And pride has been the root of all sin ever since. I used to think that self-loathing was the furthest thing from pride. After all, I wasn't loving myself, I was hating myself. Then as I progressed in my Christian maturity, I learned that self-loathing *is* a sin of pride. The red flag is the prefix *self*. As soon as we take our focus off God and put it on ourselves, the trouble starts.

Peter experienced this when he walked on water. The minute he took his eyes off of Jesus, he began to sink (see Matt. 14:29-30). Eve had it all—a sinless, perfect life where she and Adam strolled in the beautiful Garden of Eden with their Creator and all they had to do was obey God and not eat the fruit of one tree. They could have eaten the fruit from all the rest of the trees.

We don't like to be told we can't have it all. The striving, the race up the corporate ladder, the "keeping up with the Joneses" mentality in our homes—we want whatever we can get, whatever others have. The one with the most toys wins, or so we learn in childhood. One of the phrases toddlers love to say is: "Mine!" Watch little children when they are put together with their toys. They immediately start eyeing what toys the other children have and they quickly set out to get them.

Cell phone companies and computer manufacturers play right into this behavior, by constantly improving their products and coming out with new models. Growing up, our telephone (which was corded and hung on the wall) was probably at least 30 years old. And it easily would have lasted another 30 years. Today, people check their cell phone contracts to see when they are eligible for the next phone upgrade, which could be in as little as a year's time.

In Need of a Savior

Each cell phone company competes with the other, in a deafening race to have the latest applications, gadgets, and options on the phone. Are we satisfied with all of the fruit in the garden save for that one tree, or is that the one we want, because we were told that we can't have it? Just say *no* to that toddler who reaches for the toy and says, "Mine" and watch what happens.

We don't like it. And we let everyone around us know it. Now, I'm not saying that everyone is like this and as we find more peace in Christ, as we anchor ourselves more firmly to the Rock, this desire for self diminishes. But it is always under the surface, waiting to be stoked by our enemy.

When we hurt, we filter our pain through that hurt. And we want to feel better. None of this is wrong, we need to work through our feelings and then let them go. Dwelling on them only makes them worse. But when the enemy steps in, that hurt can turn into sin.

Maybe our boss passed us up for the raise. Or claimed credit for our work. We forget that God provides for our every need and that our work should be an offering to the Lord. *"Vengeance is Mine,"* God said (Rom. 12:19). But we say, "If that is the way he is going to treat me, then I am just going to leave early, I'm entitled to it." Or we may take office supplies home, as a means of compensating ourselves for the raise we did not get. Now we have just stolen and worse, we are justifying our sin. We are not owning up to it and we're not seeing the sin.

How does all of this relate to the initial pain we are in and to our feelings of worthlessness? Well, as we process the pain, we must be careful not to seek vengeance or justify our actions as we heal.

I didn't realize—and quite frankly, I didn't care—if I hurt others as I healed. I never aimed to hurt anyone else, but I was too focused on my own feelings to think about the repercussions of what my actions were doing to those around me. Whether intentionally or not, others suffered at my hand.

Finally healing enough to see this was a huge step for me. We need to be accountable to God and others for our actions. We cannot plead ignorance. I remember getting in trouble as a teenager, by doing something I didn't know was wrong. I was told: "Ignorance of the law is no excuse."

So it is with God's law. Our ignorance, our denial, our stubborn refusal to keep our eyes trained on God, will get us in trouble every time. We cannot plead ignorance in hurting others. As we advance in the healing process, there comes a time when we must make amends whenever possible.

But first, we must recognize that the other person has been hurt, too, and now has their own issues and healing to do. I think this is the truest form of the continuing cycle of abuse. We might not ever sexually abuse another person, but the emotional, physical, or psychological abuse we heap on can wreck lives just as well.

So much of my past is a blur and I see that as a Godsend. As I grow stronger and desire more to minister and help others who are suffering, God gives me small peeks into my past. It is not pretty.

In case I ever thought my memories were subjective and I was just being too harsh on myself, I have wonderful friends to gently remind me of just how far I have traveled. It is hard to hear the stories retold in their words, to be reminded of the pain I have caused them.

I can always look on the bright side and know that my children are stronger, more competent, independent, and compassionate because of what they went through. They, too, were forced to grow up faster in some ways. But they also got to experience a wonderful childhood that I never did. Their lives are a mixed canvas of having wonderful opportunities and a stable home life, but not having the closeness of a nurturing and healthy mother available to them.

I would read to them at night, but the stories were more wistful tales of what might have been than delightful recaps of laughing, silly, joyous times together. There are so many snapshots in my mind: decorating the house at Christmas, ice skating, sledding in the park… all with me on the sidelines, smiling and cheering them on. I didn't know how to get down there on the snow and ice and laugh and just let loose and enjoy.

When my kids went on a roller coaster—something I never did—I always sat on the bench next to the ride, taking pictures and waving as they careened over the hills and jostled around the turns. Sometimes I would stand in line with them to get close-up photographs of them before they took off. I would watch the ride operators bring down the thick harnesses over their bodies. I watched them snap into place, restraining my children to keep them safe from harm. As my kids loved roller coasters, this scene was replayed over and over again.

There was always something about that action that I could relate to. When the harnesses would lock into place with a heavy clicking metal sound, my heart would skip a beat. It wasn't adrenaline pumping or fear for them on the ride; it was the realization that in an intangible way, this is what I decided to do to myself a very long time ago. Stay locked into my protective cocoon, where I couldn't run free, but I was also kept safe; restrained against the fun things in life, unable to fully experience them with wild abandon.

One night, I attended a healing service at church. God really met me there and relieved a lot of the burdens and guilt I felt. Through deep healing prayer and meditation, I felt God's presence envelop me. Jesus was there also, and in my mind's eye, He waited for me to bring Him gifts. Little by little, I handed over my packages:

Healing in the Hurting Places

disappointment...sorrow...loneliness. As I gave up each gift to Him, my heart felt lighter.

When I was through, Jesus offered a gift to me. It was His unconditional love for me. My whole body radiated with the warmth of His love. I kept my eyes squeezed shut; the sensation was too wonderful to chance opening my eyes and letting the world back in. I just wanted to stay in this moment of love, peace, and joy. I can still close my eyes and recall that feeling. I remember staying in the chapel long after the service had ended, basking in that incredible feeling. Nothing in life mattered at that moment, not my past, not my present, not anything I held dear.

Paul said, *"To live is Christ, and to die is gain"* (Phil. 1:21) and at that moment, those words made perfect sense to me. They still do, but being back in the world again, I need to remind myself of how precious and simple it all is.

That night, it was late by the time I returned home after the service. It was so hard to tear myself away from the chapel and I didn't want to lose hold of that amazing feeling. But God was not finished with me yet. As I drove home, my heart was light and at peace. Cars passed me and cut me off as I drove the speed limit and I was unfazed by it all. I had nowhere to be in a hurry—and that was a radical thought for me.

When I came home, I had the inexplicable urge to kick off my sneakers and jump up and down on my bed. Which, silly as it may sound, I did. With each bounce, it was as if all of the years and restraints were being lifted off and my soul was being made light. I thought about how incredibly free, silly, and...*happy* I felt. I tried to remember when I had felt such unrestrained joy and freedom. Then it hit me. It was when I was seven years old, before I lost my innocence. Long, thick, dark, wavy hair, bouncing up and down, slapping my shoulders as I leapt and twirled. Giggling, jumping, hands flying up and down—free.

I had forgotten all about those days. What it was like not to be so serious, guarded, and driven, and how good it was to just enjoy the silliness of jumping up and down on a bed. As I rose in the air, I could be anything—a pilot, a princess, even Rapunzel with the long golden tresses, like in my storybook. The world held endless possibilities and none of it was serious. It was just play. *Play.* That was a four-letter word that no longer existed in my vocabulary.

I had forgotten how, on the day I lost my innocence, I bundled all of those carefree days of childhood and just put them away, out of sight. Or I might have given them away; I didn't have use for them anymore. I was no longer a child. There would be no more bed-jumping or dreams of princesses in flowing dresses. After the day I was raped, I never jumped on my bed again. It was as if I had forgotten how.

KEPT SAFE AFTER ALL

Jesus gave that gift back to me. He has always had a heart for children.

At that time the disciples came to Jesus and asked, "Who is the greatest in the kingdom of heaven?" He called a little child and had him stand among them. And He said: "I tell you the truth, unless you change and become like little children, you will never enter the kingdom of heaven. Therefore, whoever humbles himself like this child is the greatest in the kingdom of heaven. And whoever welcomes a little child like this in My name welcomes Me" (Matthew 18:1-5 NIV).

What a beautiful portrait of Jesus with a child gathered around Him! But He goes on to say,

Healing in the Hurting Places

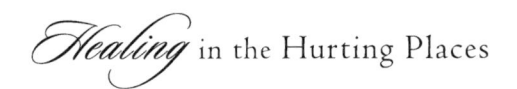

But if anyone causes one of these little ones who believe in Me to sin, it would be better for him to have a large millstone hung around his neck and to be drowned in the depths of the sea. Woe to the world because of the things that cause people to sin! Such things must come, but woe to the man through whom they come! (Matthew 18:6-7 NIV)

God does not wish harm to come to any of His children. When our hearts break, His breaks more. Sexual abuse survivors often ask, "Where is God in the midst of this?" For a long time, I questioned why God allowed the things that happened in my life. *Why had He not kept me safe as He promised?*

We are told that unless we become like little children, we cannot enter the Kingdom of Heaven, that we are to have a childlike faith. I do not believe that God is instructing us to jump up and down on our beds, but I do know that He wishes us to walk in freedom, free from the bondage of our sins and those pressed upon us by others. He wants us to experience joy in Him, not burdened down with guilt for things we have been forgiven for.

I have not jumped on my bed since, but there wasn't a need for it, either. God gave me a precious gift that night, the gift of unconditional love, purchased by the death of His Son on a cross for all of us—that supreme sacrifice, so we would no longer be shackled by sins. He had paid the price and that allowed me to release the bondage I had kept myself in all of these years. I thought I needed to pay the price for something I had done wrong; but in reality, none of us can ever pay the high price of our freedom.

There was another reason to jump for joy that night. After Jesus and I had exchanged gifts and I sat there basking in the warmth of His love, in my soul's eye, I saw Jesus off in the distance. I strained to focus on the vision, to see what Jesus had cloaked in His flowing white robes. I prayed to draw nearer, my curiosity mounting.

And as I drew closer, I could see a little girl with long, dark hair. She was eight years old. Jesus had His arms wrapped around her, protecting her. In my heart, I once again heard those familiar words: *I will keep you safe.*

God had indeed protected and kept me safe all of those years. It never seemed to be true, because I could only look at the abuse that was thrust upon me…the trials and difficult situations I faced…all the negative lies that satan gladly whispered in my ear.

And then, as if a veil had been lifted from my heart, I understood.

God had not been keeping me safe from others' abuse or harm; He had been keeping me safe *from me*. I had been my own worst enemy all of those years. All of the striving and proving and driving to do things in my own strength were death to my soul. I had punished myself with food and I had attempted to take my own life. I berated myself and failed to love myself. I was not willing to forgive myself.

He had kept me safe until I realized that I could not do it on my own. I had believed the ultimate lies of most children who have been sexually abused. I was convinced that:

Somehow, it was all my fault.

I was bad inside.

I deserved what happened to me.

If we truly got what we deserved, none of us would have the opportunity for eternal life. Our sins would keep us separated from God. But God sent His Son, Jesus, to pay the price for our sins. Our Lord and Savior has set us free. He offers this precious gift of eternal life to

Healing in the Hurting Places

each one of us. We just need to believe in Him with a childlike faith, confess our sins and ask for His forgiveness.

My Savior not only kept me safe, but bought my freedom. I was no longer in bondage to the sin of abuse that had been thrust upon me. I was no longer held in bondage by the enemy from the aftereffects of that abuse. The child I thought had been lost had been protected by Jesus all of these years. And now that child was ready to come home.

Jesus said, "Let the little children come to Me, and do not hinder them, for the kingdom of heaven belongs to such as these"... (Matthew 19:14 NIV).

Appendix A

What (and What Not) to Say to a Sexual-Abuse Victim

Even the most well-intentioned folks may struggle with what to say to someone who is a victim of sexual abuse. Just like when someone dies, we want to say something to the bereaved, but often we don't know the right words to use.

I want to inject a note of caution here. The following is not a legalist list of do's and don'ts, but merely a guide to help. Where the person is in the healing process makes a difference; it has an impact on what they are ready to hear. But overall, certain guidelines can be followed so as not to exacerbate the wound.

A victim, above all else, needs to know that they are not to blame and what happened was not their fault. They are probably already wrestling with guilt, blame, and shame; and reinforcing this is detrimental to healing.

If you are unsure of what to say, just remember that your presence is often more than enough. Many times, the victims have no one to

Healing in the Hurting Places

turn to, feel that they will not be believed, and continue to suffer in silence. Just providing an ear to listen so they can express what is on their hearts can be the best gift you can offer. Allowing them to speak their pain and not be judged is very empowering. Even if you say nothing and let them do all of the talking, it will be a wonderful step in their healing process.

As you read the suggestions below, please note that this is by no means a complete list, and one size does not fit all. When in doubt, just let God be your guide and allow the victim to choose his or her own comfort level.

Beware of making strong suggestions as to *how* the victim should heal. This guidance should not be given unless you are a trained counselor, know the victim really well and have been with him or her through this healing process, or are certain God is truly prompting you.

For example, do not tell a victim that "he or she should not be dwelling on this." Victims will need to relive and go through the process many times until their heart begins to heal and they can handle things better. Very few are equipped from the outside to know when this time is. Healing is a very individual process, and while there may come a point when the victim needs to be told the truth in love, I would really caution anyone from feeling they can make this judgment on their own. It is usually best to let God and the victim determine the timetable that is right for them.

In the meantime, your willingness to listen, your emotional and spiritual support, and just being there for the victim is often the best help you can offer. Victims often believe that others will abandon or even abuse them, so to come alongside them and not judge them and be available to them will go a long way in helping them defeat the lies of the enemy.

What (and What Not) to Say to a Sexual-Abuse Victim

I will warn you, however, that it will not be easy to be in this position, so know that going in. The person may describe things graphically that they need to give voice to; it may be hard to listen to. They may take their pain, anger, or hurt out on you, and you must realize that it is not being directed to you, even though you might be the recipient. Being allowed to release these feelings, sometimes for the first time in their lives, is very freeing and also hard to control at first. As hard as it may be to believe this, they are not intentionally trying to take things out on you or hurt you in any way; they just don't know how to harness these feelings for the first time.

You will probably witness a seesaw of emotions if you are very close to the sexual-abuse victim on a regular basis. He or she may appear to be getting better and then experience a devastating setback. This is all part of the healing process; do not be discouraged, and please do not make the person feel bad for slipping back. Sometimes there is a lot of "one step, forward, two steps back" in healing.

What Not to Say to a Victim

- *I know how you feel.* Unless you have also been abused, you cannot know exactly how the victim feels.

- *This happened a long time ago—you need to let it go.* Healing is an individual timetable. Some people take 20, 30, or even 40 years to start coming to terms with this. They will "let it go" when they are healed and ready.

- *You need to put this in the past and stop thinking about it.* A victim may have been told a lot of things at the time of the abuse, such as, "Don't tell," "This feels good," "This is what love is," etc. They now have to sort through all of these false messages. Telling them now what they should be thinking (or not thinking) is a form of control that the victim does not need to experience again.

- *I thought you were past all of this.* This makes the person feel guilty or bad for disappointing you. It sets up a principle that you are dictating the healing timetable.

- *"That's not normal / You're crazy / I thought you were a Christian"* (or any variation that implies the person is not acting the way that he or she should. Victims already feel shame, embarrassment, being singled-out, and the last thing they want is to stand out any further. They also typically blame themselves or have self-hatred. So telling them that they are not normal or not acting in a normal manner or seem to be crazy only reinforces these negative self-images. And we are not the "faith police." That is between them and God.)

- *If you forgive the perpetrator, you'll feel better.* Forgiveness is a loaded issue and is only part of the healing process. Plus, you do not know what will or will not make that individual feel better; this is the victim's healing journey, not yours.

- *You must have done something to provoke this.* This will only compound feelings of guilt and shame. Rape is a crime of control and sometimes rage; it has little or nothing to do with sex. Victims should never be made to feel that they were the cause in any way.

- *Now that you've told me, you can forget about it.* Telling usually opens the door, especially in the beginning. Now the victim is ready to take the next steps. But even if the victim is sharing this with you long after being healed, please know that it is something he or she will never forget about. The healed victim may not think about it every day; it may no longer be

What (and What Not) to Say to a Sexual-Abuse Victim

bothersome; but the person who suffered sexual abuse will always remember it.

- *Why didn't you stop it?* The victim often feels powerless or too paralyzed at the time to protect and defend against the perpetrator. What can a child of four do against a stronger, heavier adult? Please do not make the victim feel at fault.

- *Why didn't you tell someone sooner?* You may never know how hard it was for the victim to tell you now. Be grateful that he or she is now venturing forth and trusting you enough to share something this painful.

- *"Boys will be boys," "That's how men are,"* or any variation of this theme. These statements are often said out of ignorance or an attempt to make the victim feel better. It just diminishes the crime and does nothing to address the seriousness or heart of the matter. It is also unfair to blast a gender when the truth is that perpetrators can be of either gender, any race or religion, and a variety of ages. Generalization is never the right approach to an individual issue. The issue is the person in front of you who is in pain. He or she needs to remain your focus.

- *Were you raped? Did he penetrate you?* It is up to the victim to share whatever details she feels comfortable discussing. Asking a victim for details is akin to asking the bereaved how their loved one died. If she wants to fill you in, she will. But asking can make the victim feel very uncomfortable. I remember breaking the news to someone; I remember how difficult it was and how all the listener wanted were the details. I felt like saying, "This is not a romance novel or exposé; this is my life. I am hurting and in pain here; this is not about addressing your morbid curiosity."

Healing in the Hurting Places

What to Say to a Victim

- *I'm sorry for what happened to you.* This is one of the most important things you can say to a victim. Said with sincerity, it should be the first thing out of your mouth. To validate a victim's experience is incredibly empowering and healing. Sadly, not enough victims ever hear this.

- *I'm here for you.* Just being there physically and emotionally can be very healing.

- *I'm happy to listen to whatever you are comfortable in sharing.* Always allow the victim to dictate the pace and comfort level. Some may want to go into detail; others may struggle with even vaguely revealing any part of what happened.

- *I will pray for you.* If you feel led in this direction, prayer can often be the best help you can offer.

- *This wasn't your fault. You are not to blame.* It helps to let the victim know that he or she is not to blame, because they may be wrestling with self-doubt. Also, this allows victims to feel more comfortable in trusting you, as you are not holding them responsible or making them feel worse for what happened.

- *This doesn't change anything between us.* Whether you are a spouse, a co-worker, or a friend, the victim needs the security of knowing this information will not cause you to treat him or her any differently. Victims fear being judged, pushed away, or even thought of differently once the truth is out. It is important to assure them that what happened to them does not change your relationship.

What (and What Not) to Say to a Sexual-Abuse Victim

YOU MAY ALSO...

- Accompany them to the hospital and/or police department.

- Encourage them to call a hotline, like RAINN, when they are ready.

- Offer them a hug. But be sensitive to the fact that they were a victim of a crime involving unwanted touch and they may not want or be receptive to being touched, even with a caring hug, at this stage in their recovery. Ask for permission first.

IF A CHILD TELLS YOU THAT THEY HAVE BEEN/ARE BEING ABUSED...

- Listen to what they have to say—do not be judgmental or ask leading questions.

- Be calm; it may be difficult for you to hear what they are telling you, but it is harder for them to tell. You need to be the strong one in the situation if you can be.

- Assure the child that it was not their fault.

- Believe them and confirm whatever feelings they are having—fear, disgust, anger, etc.

- Determine if the child is in any immediate danger. Is their home safe to return to?

- Let them know that you are glad that they told you.

- Assure them that this doesn't change your relationship with them. An abused child may fear they won't be believed or that you will think differently about them because of what happened.

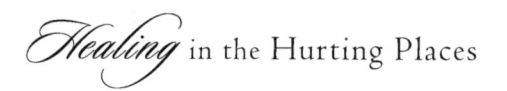

- Be honest with the child and let them know what you are planning to do (call the police, etc.) so they won't feel betrayed by finding out afterward that you told someone else. Let them know that you will try to find help for them from people who know how to handle this.

Appendix B

Resources

The following is a list of resources and organizations where you can obtain further information and, in some cases, help and/or counsel. The information is accurate as of the time of publication, but resources change over time and this does not represent a complete list of all that may be available. Many churches offer resources that may not be publicly known. The inclusion of an organization on this list does not imply an endorsement from the author or publisher, but merely a source that deals with the topic of abuse.

A note about these organizations: Some are staffed by volunteers; all are staffed by humans. If we are in crisis, we hope that the person on the other end of the phone will be trained, compassionate, and able to help us. Most of the time, this will be true, but we are all human and results may vary. If you do not find what you are looking for on the first call and need help, please do not give up. There are many organizations out there to assist. Please keep trying until you find the right fit or answer. And if you do receive help, please consider giving back when you are able. Many of these organizations are short-staffed and under-financed. Financial support, volunteering,

Healing in the Hurting Places

even just calling or dropping a note to say that they helped will go a long way to encouraging those who staff these places.

1in6
(for male survivors of sexual abuse)
www.1in6.org

Alcoholics Anonymous
A.A. World Services, Inc., 11th Floor
475 Riverside Drive at West 120th St.
New York, NY 10115
212-870-3400
www.aa.org

Darkness to Light's National Helpline Network
866-FOR-LIGHT
www.darkness2light.org
www.dahmw.org

Male Survivor
www.malesurvivor.org

Narcotics Anonymous
PO Box 9999
Van Nuys, California 91409
818-773-9999
www.na.org

National Center for Missing and Exploited Children
800.843.5678

National Center for Victims of Crime, Abuse, Domestic Violence, Rape – Information & Referrals
2000 M Street NW, Suite 480
Washington, DC 20036
800-FYI-CALL (800.394.2255)
TTY/TDD: 1-800-211-7996
www.ncvc.org

National Child Abuse Hotline (24-hour)
800-422-4453

Resources

National Clearinghouse on Marital & Date Rape
2325 Oak Street
Berkeley, CA 94708
http://ncmdr.org

National Crime Victims Research and Treatment Center
Medical University of South Carolina
165 Cannon Street, P.O. Box 250852
Charleston, SC 29425-0742
843-792-8209
colleges.musc.edu/ncvc

National Domestic Violence Hotline (24 hour)
800-799-SAFE • 800.787.3224 (TTY)
www.ojp.usdoj.gov/ovc/help/hotline/welcome.html

National Runaway Switchboard
800.621.4000

National STD Hotline
800.227.8922

National Sexual Violence Resource Center
123 North Enola Drive
Enola, Pennsylvania 17025
877-739-3895 • TTY: 717-909-0715
www.nsvrc.org

National Teen Dating Abuse Helpline
866-331-9474 • 1-866-331-8453 (TTY)
http://www.loveisrespect.org

New Life Ministries
PO Box 1018
Laguna Beach, CA 92652-1018
800-NEW-LIFE
www.newlife.com

Overeaters Anonymous, Inc. (OA)
PO Box 44020
Rio Rancho, NM 87174-4020
505-891-2664
www.oa.org

Healing in the Hurting Places

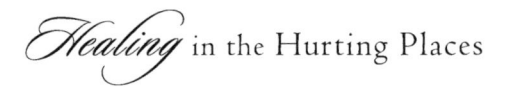

Rape, Abuse & Incest National Network (RAINN)
2000 L Street, NW Suite 406
Washington, DC 20036
202-544-3064
www.rainn.org

Rescued & Redeemed
(for advocacy and education on sex trafficking)
888.400.1571
info@rescuedredeemed.org
www.rescuedredeemed.org

Safe Horizon
800-621-HOPE
www.safehorizon.org

Sexual Assault Hotline
1-800-656-HOPE (4673)

Speaking Out About Rape, Inc. (SOAR)
3208 E. Colonial Drive Unit 243
Orlando, FL 32803
321-278-5246
www.soar99.org

Stop It Now
888-PREVENT
www.stopitnow.org

National Suicide Prevention Lifeline
800-273-TALK

Survivors of Incest Anonymous World Service Office
PO Box 190
Benson, MD 21018-9998
410-893-3322
www.siawso.org

Suicide Hotline
800-273-TALK

National Suicide Crisis Hotline
800.SUICIDE (784.2433)

Resources

XXXchurch
(For help with pornography issues)
http://xxxchurch.com

STATE RESOURCES

ALABAMA
Alabama Coalition Against Rape
334-264-0123
www.acar.org

ALASKA
Alaska Network on Domestic Violence
& Sexual Assault (ANDVSA)
907-586-3650 (Juneau)
907-747-7545 (Sitka)
www.andvsa.org

ARIZONA
Arizona Sexual Assault Network (AzSAN)
www.arizonasexualassaultnetwork.org

ARKANSAS
Arkansas Coalition Against Sexual Assault
866-63-ACASA (22272)
www.acasa.us

CALIFORNIA
California Coalition Against Sexual Assault (CALCASA)
916-446-2520
www.calcasa.org

COLORADO
Colorado Coalition Against Sexual Assault
303.839.9999
www. ccasa.org

CONNECTICUT
Connecticut Sexual Assault Crisis Services (CONNSACS)
860-282-9881
www.connsacs.org

Healing in the Hurting Places

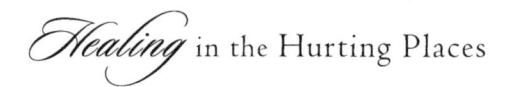

DELAWARE
Contact Delaware
302-761-9800
www.contactdelaware.org

FLORIDA
Florida Council Against Sexual Violence
850-297-2000
www.fcasv.org

GEORGIA
Georgia Network to End Sexual Assault (GNESA)
404-815-5261 • 1-866-354-3672
www.gnesa.org

HAWAII
Sex Abuse Treatment Center
808-524-RAPE (7273)
www.satchawaii.com

IDAHO
Idaho Coalition Against Sexual & Domestic Violence (ICASDV)
208-384-0419

ILLINOIS
Illinois Coalition Against Sexual Assault (ICASA)
217-753-4117
www.icasa.org

INDIANA
Indiana Coalition Against Sexual Assault
317-423-0233
www.incasa.org

IOWA
Iowa Coalition Against Sexual Assault (ICASA)
515-244-7424
www.iowacasa.org

KANSAS
Kansas Coalition Against Sexual and Domestic Violence
785-232-9784
www.kcsdv.org

Resources

KENTUCKY
Kentucky Association of Sexual Assault Programs
502-226-2704
http://kyasap.brinkster.net

LOUISIANA
Louisiana Foundation Against Sexual Assault (LAFASA)
985-345-5995

MAINE
Maine Coalition Against Sexual Assault (MECASA)
207-626-0034

MARYLAND
Maryland Coalition Against Sexual Assault—Arnold, MD
410-974-4507
www.mcasa.org

MASSACHUSETTS
Jane Doe Inc./MCASADV
617-248-0922

New England Learning Center for Women in Transition
479 Main St.
Greenfield, MA 01302
413-772-0871
www.nelcwit.org

Rape Crisis Center of Central Massachusetts
800-870-5905
www.rapecrisiscenter.org

MICHIGAN
Michigan Coalition Against Domestic & Sexual Violence
517-347-7000
www.mcadsv.org

MINNESOTA
Minnesota Coalition Against Sexual Assault—Minneapolis, MN
651-209-9993
www.mncasa.org

Healing in the Hurting Places

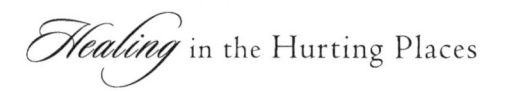

MISSISSIPPI
Mississippi Coalition Against Domestic Violence
601-981-9196
www.mcadv.org

MISSOURI
Missouri Coalition Against Sexual Assault (MoCASA)
573-636-8776
www.mssu.edu/missouri/mocasa/mocasa.htm

MONTANA
Montana Coalition Against Domestic & Sexual Violence
406-443-7794
www.mcadsv.com

NEBRASKA
Nebraska Domestic Violence Sexual Assault Coalition
402-476-6256
www.ndvsac.org

NEVADA
The Rape Crisis Center of Southern Nevada (24-hour)
702-366-1640
www.therapecrisiscenter.org

Nevada Coalition Against Sexual Violence
702-990-3460
http://ncasv.org/?page_id=52

NEW HAMPSHIRE
New Hampshire Coalition Against Domestic & Sexual Violence/
New Beginnings/A Women's Crisis Center
1-866-644-3574 (Domestic Violence)
1-800-277-5570 (Sexual Assault)
www.nhcadsv.org
www.newbeginningsnh.org

NEW JERSEY
New Jersey Coalition Against Sexual Assault
800-601-7200
www.njcasa.org

Resources

NEW MEXICO
New Mexico Coalition of Sexual Assault Programs
505-883-8020

NEW YORK
Coercion, Rape, & Surviving
120 Richmond Quad
University at Buffalo
Buffalo, NY 14261
716-645-2720
ub-counseling.buffalo.edu/violenceoverview.shtml

New York State Coalition Against Sexual Assault
518-482-4222
www.nyscasa.org

NORTH CAROLINA
North Carolina Coalition Against Sexual Assault
919-871-1015
www.nccasa.net

NORTH DAKOTA
North Dakota Council on Abused Women's Services (NDCAWS)/Coalition Against Sexual Assault in North Dakota (CASAND)
701-255-6240
www.ndcaws.org

OHIO
Ohio Coalition on Sexual Assault
933 High Street, Suite 120B
Worthington, OH 43085
614-781-1902

OKLAHOMA
Oklahoma Coalition Against
Domestic Violence and Sexual Assault
800-522-7233
www.ocadvsa.org

Healing in the Hurting Places

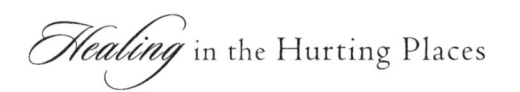

OREGON
Oregon Coalition Against Domestic and Sexual Violence
503.230.1951
www.ocadsv.com

PENNSYLVANIA
Pennsylvania Coalition Against Rape (PCAR)
717-728-9740
Toll-free hotline: 800-692-7445
www.pcar.org

RHODE ISLAND
The Sexual Assault & Trauma Resource Center (SATRC)
401-421-4100

SOUTH CAROLINA
South Carolina Coalition Against Domestic Violence & Sexual Abuse
803-256-2900
www.sccadvasa.org

SOUTH DAKOTA
South Dakota Coalition Against Domestic Violence and Sexual Assault
605-945-0869
www.sdcadvsa.org

TENNESSEE
Tennessee Coalition Against Domestic & Sexual Violence
615-386-9406
www.tcadsv.org

TEXAS
Texas Association Against Sexual Assault—Austin, TX
512-474-7190
www.taasa.org

UTAH
Utah Coalition Against Sexual Assault (UCASA)
801-746-0404
www.ucasa.org

Resources

VERMONT
Vermont Network Against
Domestic Violence and Sexual Assault
802-223-1302

VIRGINIA
Virginians Aligned Against Sexual Assault
804-979-9002

WASHINGTON
Washington Coalition of Sexual Assault Programs
360-754-7583
www.wcsap.org

WASHINGTON, DC
DC Rape Crisis Center
202-232-0789
www.dcrcc.org

WEST VIRGINIA
West Virginia Foundation for Rape Information and Services
304-366-9500
www.fris.org

WISCONSIN
Wisconsin Coalition Against Sexual Assault
608-257-1516
www.wcasa.org

Asha Family Services
414-875-1511
www.ashafamilyservices.com

WYOMING
Coalition Against Domestic Violence & Sexual Assault
307-755-5481

About Karen F. Riley

Karen F. Riley has been writing since she was eight years old. She was nationally published at the age of eleven. Since then, Karen has written for newspapers and magazines. She has authored three weekly newspaper columns and three books:

Whispers in the Pines: The Secrets of Colliers Mills

Voices in the Pines: True Stories from the New Jersey Pine Barrens

Images of America: The Pine Barrens of New Jersey

Karen has been married to Bill for 31 years and they are the proud parents of three children: Lisa, Laura, and Christopher. They reside in the rural town of New Egypt, New Jersey.

After 20 years in the corporate world, in seven different fields, and having survived four layoffs, she started her own business. KFR Communications, LLC—a custom graphic and Website design company she owns with her business partner, Andrew Gioulis—is now in its eighth year of operations. For most of her life, Karen measured her success by what she achieved in her own strength. Then on July 24, 2005, that world and belief system was rocked when she accepted Jesus as her Lord and Savior.

Augustine said, "You have made us for yourself, O Lord, and our hearts are restless until they rest in you."

Karen began to understand why God blessed her with the gift of writing and speaking and how she could glorify Him with it. She began writing as a means to deal with the pain of childhood sexual abuse. Today, she heads up a ministry called "Healing in the Hurting Places" to offer hope to those suffering in the same way. This book is part of that journey.

For more information, please log onto: www.healinginthehurtingplaces.org.

IN THE RIGHT HANDS, THIS BOOK WILL CHANGE LIVES!

Most of the people who need this message will not be looking for this book. To change their lives, you need to put a copy of this book in their hands.

> *But others (seeds) fell into good ground, and brought forth fruit, some a hundred-fold, some sixty-fold, some thirty-fold* (Matthew 13:8).

Our ministry is constantly seeking methods to find the good ground, the people who need this anointed message to change their lives. Will you help us reach these people?

> *Remember this—a farmer who plants only a few seeds will get a small crop. But the one who plants generously will get a generous crop* (2 Corinthians 9:6).

**EXTEND THIS MINISTRY BY SOWING
3 BOOKS, 5 BOOKS, 10 BOOKS, OR MORE TODAY,
AND BECOME A LIFE CHANGER!**

Thank you,

Don Nori Sr., Founder
Destiny Image
Since 1982

Destiny Image

DESTINY IMAGE PUBLISHERS, INC.

"Speaking to the Purposes of God for This Generation and for the Generations to Come."

VISIT OUR NEW SITE HOME AT
WWW.DESTINYIMAGE.COM

FREE SUBSCRIPTION TO DI NEWSLETTER

Receive free unpublished articles by top DI authors, exclusive discounts, and free downloads from our best and newest books.
Visit www.destinyimage.com to subscribe.

Write to: Destiny Image
                P.O. Box 310
                Shippensburg, PA 17257-0310

Call: 1-800-722-6774

Email: orders@destinyimage.com

For a complete list of our titles or to place an order online, visit www.destinyimage.com.

FIND US ON FACEBOOK OR FOLLOW US ON TWITTER.

www.facebook.com/destinyimage   **facebook**
www.twitter.com/destinyimage   **twitter**